Spiritual Ass Kicker's

BOOM BOOK

Ignite Your Intentions And Create Blazing Results

Amy Scott Grant, MBA

Spiritual Ass Kicker

Castle Rock, CO

Published by Liberto Press

Castle Rock, Colorado, USA

Although the author and publisher have made every effort to ensure that the information in this book was correct at press time, the author and publisher do not assume and hereby disclaim any liability to any party for any loss, damage, or disruption caused by errors or omissions, whether such errors or omissions result from negligence, accident, or any other cause. Please remember to drink plenty of water when performing or receiving any kind of energy work or healing.

ISBN: 978-0-9974466-5-4

Liberto Press fifth edition, November 2018

www.AskAmyAnything.com

DEDICATION

This book is dedicated to The Creator,

who ignites the divine spark in each of us…

and lights a fire under our butts when necessary.

Let's set aside the fact (for now) that you are divinely perfect, and you don't technically "need" anything to be complete. Having said that, there are countless "things" that, once added to your life, will enhance, expedite, ignite, or otherwise enrich your experience of life and how you move through it.

The Boom Book is one of those things.

Since my mid-twenties, I've been getting shockingly good results by creating a focused vision for the coming year. Did you just ask me how long ago that was? What? Sorry, you're breaking up. I can't hear you. Let's move on. Over the years, I've shared bits and pieces here and there with my clients, but *2015 Boom* was the first time I shared the entire process. By pre-planning your intention and clarifying what it will take to get you there, you are statistically ten times more likely to achieve your intentions than someone who just thinks about it or talks about it. And let's not even mention all those New Year's resolutions that never saw the light of February.

Here's how this book can help:

The Boom Book (I call it "Boom," for short) is a *personal almanac* for your year. We are in this together, you and I, and we'll take a unique approach to balance by relying on the chakra system to lead you through an intentional mapping of your year, laying the groundwork for future years to come.

The word **almanac** refers to an annual calendar that includes pertinent information for the year. For example, a farmer's almanac includes tide tables, key dates for the growing season, moon tables, etc. Your almanac (this workbook, once you complete it) will feature the intentions, the vision, the clarity, and the actions you require to create the year that you really want. The Boom process will help you to gain clarity around your desires and your needs, and then map them into a format that will expedite and facilitate manifestation of those desires in the next twelve months.

The beauty of this approach is that you can start any time—no need to wait for a Monday, or the first of the month, or January, or your birthday, or any of those silly things we all do. You can work through this almanac at your own pace, and best of all, you will do this **just once** for an entire year. Once you complete this workbook, your vision will be clear, your action steps will be set, and all that's left is for you to simply move as you are guided. I know that when you see the results you've created, you'll want to repeat this process year after year.

Before we get started, let me tell you a little about who I am and why I know such things.

I'm a master intuitive healer, Spiritual Ass Kicker, irreverently entertaining speaker, multi-time bestselling author, and badass thought leader. I have cleared millions of blocks for thousands of women (and maybe a couple hundred men) across twenty-nine countries. I have created dozens of powerful programs and premium courses (and a handful of f'amazing books) and I get jaw-dropping results for teachers, accountants, sales professionals, entrepreneurs, moms, executives, coaches, artists, analysts, healers, and others just like you.

My full bio (including a special invitation that may or may not be for you) is in the *About the Author* section at the end of this book.

But enough about me, let's talk about you.

Are you ready to lay the foundation for your best year yet? Ready to clarify your vision and crystallize your intention? Are you ready to create a powerful strategic plan to roll out a truly transformational twelve months? Are you ready to start this day with passion, purpose, and focus?

Then buckle up because this simple workbook has the capacity to rock your socks as you consciously create a powerhouse year!

Level 1: Induction

Amazing! Miraculous! Extraordinary!

When you operate your life mindfully with *intention,* you will produce results that blow the minds of people around you. The truly exquisite thing is that it's not hard. You're taking the first big steps right now, simply by using this personal almanac.

This first level is called **Induction** because we are creating a foundation and giving rise to something.

The Purpose of this Book

The purpose of this workbook is to add more "Boom" into your life for the next twelve months. The best part is that **you** get to define "Boom," beginning with our very first exercise. But first, let's address some of the questions you may have.

Why Be Intentional?

Without intentionality, your life operates like a ship lost at sea. You are tossed about on the waves of whim, and sadly, this is how most people move through life. Yet, you are here because you want more. You know that it's reasonable and fair for you to demand more from life, and this simple workbook will help you get it.

By being intentional about your year, you are setting the pace, the feel, the atmosphere, and the end result. You are powerful beyond belief, and it is my intention that by the time you complete this almanac, you will be far more aware of your personal power as you slide into the captain's seat and begin to steer your life mindfully and with focused intention.

Why Use this Book?

This is not the only book of its kind. However, it is the only book that combines these three key ingredients: the power and clarity of mindfully mapping out your year; the added enhancement of harnessing the chakra system to access your infinite energy; plus the direct, straightforward, and entertaining style of the Spiritual Ass Kicker.

In this book, you can expect to be guided, amused, and empowered, without any "fluff."

This book is exactly as long as it needs to be. Every exercise presented within these pages is here to move you closer to the achievement of your goals.

This book is different from a day planner because we're not mapping out the minutia of each day-to-day action here. Rather, we're creating a vision for your year.

Like Stephen Covey suggests, we are beginning with the end in mind. This allows you to create a truly powerful intention, and to allow events and opportunities to align with the desires you've set.

Why Does a Personal Almanac Work?

It may seem too good to be true. Can you really just write down a bunch of stuff and then watch in amazement as the stars and planets align to make it happen? Here's the crazy thing: even those who have had trouble manifesting what they want find *this* process to be miraculously effective.

For starters, this personal almanac creates clarity, which is half the battle. Once you know where you're going, it's a helluva lot easier to get there. So we will begin by creating personal clarity for what you want for these next twelve months.

The second major advantage of this book is that it embeds intentions and positivity into your subconscious mind. Your mind is a powerful supercomputer and you can put it to work to solve problems and help you with manifestation, without having to consciously *do* stuff all the time. By taking the time to invest in the completion of this almanac, you are cementing your desires deeply into your mind, which puts your supercomputer to work to bring you opportunities and access to everything you decide you want.

The third huge advantage to this personal almanac is it provides you with a written record of what you want. If you're anything like me, your short-term memory is crapola, which means I have no idea what I declared I wanted a year ago today (or…two months ago, or for breakfast this morning). But I can flip back to my written notes any time I wish to gain a clear and instantaneous understanding of what I was thinking around this time last year.

As you progress through this almanac workbook, you will undoubtedly find many more advantages to the Boom process, but most people find that these three major helps are enough of a motivation to get started and to work their way through to completion.

Don't be discouraged about this process if you've set New Year's resolutions that have never panned out. Most people's resolutions have fizzled out by Valentine's Day. That's why they call them **New** Year's resolutions and not **all** year resolutions.

We're not built to maintain hyper focus for months at a stretch, especially without a long-term vision. But resolutions are rarely about the vision; they're about quick results, and such half-cocked schemes seldom work.

Most people say they want to lose weight, stop smoking, and get organized. As if getting organized was a one-time thing, and as if it were that easy to quit smoking! If it were easy to quit and you could do it any time you made a resolution, we wouldn't have to hound our kids never to start in the first place. Nicotine is addictive. Just like mindless eating, negative thinking, self-criticism, and clutter.

This almanac has the power to fix your life in a year or less, but not if you think of it as a way to keep track of New Year's resolutions. This process is different, and it works at a different level within you. But most importantly, *it works,* period.

About the Chakra System

If you ask most people what they want more of in the coming year, one of the top answers you'd hear is "balance." The Boom process will help you achieve balance while achieving your goals and desires.

There are channels of energy that run inside your body at the energetic level, also called the subtle body. Many chakras exist but when you hear talk of the "chakra system," this is usually in reference to the seven main chakras (as pictured below, bottom to top): root, sacral, solar plexus, heart, throat, third eye, and crown.

If you have any experience with energy work or energy healing, you already know how important it is to keep the chakras open and balanced, otherwise illness or other issues can occur.

Balancing the chakras is a relatively simple process, but **it's not permanent.** Think of it as hydration. You'll never be "finished" drinking water because the body needs constant hydration in order to perform its essential processes. Drink as much water as you want now, and you will still grow thirsty again later, and eventually need more water. The same is true when you balance your chakras. Balanced, open chakras feel wonderful, but through the course of living life day to day, you will soon need to rebalance the chakras again.

We will use the basic principles of the chakras to design and balance your intentional plan for the year, thereby creating balance in your life and among your chakras.

Normally, chakra balancing is done from bottom to top, and as we get into the nuances of each chakra, you will understand why it is done that way. (Think: Maslow's hierarchy of needs.) But in this personal almanac, we will begin with the end in mind, as is done with any effective *intentionality* work. Therefore, we will begin at the top with the crown chakra and work our way down to the root. Call me a rebel, but it works.

Whether you are an expert on the chakra system or a total noob (or anywhere in-between), you **can** do this. Chakras can be used in countless ways, but for the purposes of this book, we will use the chakra system as a guide. Which means we will cover only what you need to know to use the chakras effectively to enhance the next year of your life.

How to Use this Book

In classic Spiritual Ass Kicker style, you will be led through a series of exercises designed to create "a-ha" moments and epiphanies. Once you get clarity, the next step is to express it in simple, powerful words and phrases. I'll walk you through all of it, step by step. We will create a single word or very short phrase to "pre-frame" your year. Once you've selected this **BOOM word**, everything else will come into focus as you complete the workbook, and we will create an effective plan of action. As I guide you through the rest of the book, you will be amazed at how quickly it all comes together in your mind and the sense of peace you gain by the time you complete this almanac. Even before you finish the last page, you will be set for the next twelve months and the magic can begin.

Do not be surprised if the first several exercises feel a bit slow or plodding. This is normal until you get the whack of clarity. I promise you, once clarity strikes, things will really speed up and the rest of the exercises will zoom by. When I was in graduate school, I read an Evelyn Wood speed-reading book. The first two chapters took me forever to read (although in reality, it was probably only about forty minutes), but once I got a handle on the first couple of speed-reading exercises, the rest of the book zipped by. The Boom process works in a similar way.

I realize we live in an all-digital, all-the-time kind of society, but trust me when I tell you that this is the least effective method for intentional work. There are many benefits in hand-writing the words.

For starters, writing out words in longhand accesses a different part of the brain than typing on a keyboard. (Nope, it's still a different part of the brain than dictating, but nice try.) Writing words will lodge them into your memory in a way that typing just can't.

Additionally, when you are writing, you are accessing more of your senses. There's the smell of the ink or the pencil lead, the soft scratching sound of the writing implement dragging across the paper, the feel of the pen or pencil in your hand, and the visual aspect of being able to see the words as they are created by your dominant hand. Yes, taste may even get involved if you are a cap chewer or perhaps the odd individual who likes to lick the pencil before beginning to write. (Eww.)

So even though you may feel resistant, I challenge you to pick up a pen or pencil and write everything in this workbook longhand. You might curse me now, but you'll thank me later when your dreams have manifested in strange and wonderful ways.

Once you finish the book, don't file it *too* far away, as you will want to trot it out periodically to check your progress.

How Long Will It Take to Complete the Almanac?

That all depends on you, friend. My advice is to start right now and get as far into it as you can. You've been waiting for this book and now it's here in your hands, so why not strike while the iron is hot?

Work as much as you can today, and then you may wish to carve out an hour or two per day over the next several days. I love this process, and find it exhilarating and energizing. So I tend to work through it as quickly as I can, usually over three to five days. But you may be the type of person who needs more time to think and to process, in which case it may take you as long as a couple of weeks. There's no wrong way to work through this book—just dive right in.

Can I Skip Around?

The almanac works best when you work it from start to finish, without skipping around. As you dive in, you'll quickly notice how each section builds on the last.

You can use this workbook for business and for personal use. You are welcome to complete only the exercises and processes that apply to you, although I would invite you to consider that they *all* apply to you. But for example, if you are a stay-at-home mom who is a full-time domestic goddess, then you may wish to skip over the business worksheets. Unless of course, you've decided that this is your year to finally start your plan for global economic domination, in which case it helps to get clarity around what kind of business or earning potential you could create.

Everything in this book works.

Not just for me, but for countless others, and it can work for you, too. Having said that, no one here will be judging you or calling you bad or wrong for skipping pages or exercises. It's your year. If you're anything like me, you want to squeeze every drop out of life, so you'll work through every exercise.

But you are an individual who is ultimately responsible for your success and your outcomes, and therefore, you can **complete this book in whatever way feels most optimal to you.**

Of course, don't expect jaw-dropping results if you read this introduction and then think "I'll work on this later" and then let the book spend the next eleven months collecting dust on the shelf. You know the drill; you get out of it what you put into it. It's only a cliché because it's true. Let's get started.

Did You Know?

I moved my family to Colorado after Hurricane Katrina but **not** because of flooding. Our home was the only house in our neighborhood that didn't flood. The floodwater rose within inches of our front door.

About six months before the storm, I set an intention that we'd sell the house and get a lot more than we paid for it.

Yep, that's the power of intentionality.

When I talk about "Boom" in the context of this book, I'm referring to adding more pizzazz, punch, and spice into your life, like the noise a firework shell makes when it explodes.

Let's take stock of your life right now and benchmark some Boom. For each of the questions below, answer as "Boom" or "meh" or "yuck," depending on how you feel about that topic. Count the booms in each category to see how different parts of your life measure up on the Boom scale. Skip any categories that are not applicable to you.

Feel like something important wasn't mentioned? Go ahead and use the last row at the bottom of each chart to fill in your own measure of satisfaction.

For the chart called "Your Family," I'm leaving it up to you how you'd like to interpret that. It could mean your birth family, your current family (children and/or spouse), the people who are so close to you that you consider them to be family, or any combination thereof.

YOUR WORK LIFE	BOOM	MEH	YUCK
Do you get excited when it's time to start work?			
Do you happily try to squeeze in extra stuff at the end of the work week?			
How do you feel about what you do for a living?			
How do you feel about what you earn currently?			
How do you feel about the people you work with?			
How do you feel about your current clients or customers?			
If you could get paid to do anything, how likely would you be to keep doing what you're doing?			
Total WORK LIFE Booms:			

YOUR SEX LIFE	BOOM	MEH	YUCK
How do you feel about sex in general?			
If you have a partner, how do you feel about your partner sexually?			
How satisfied do you typically feel during sex?			
How good do you feel after sex?			
Are you loving and tender with your own body?			
How attracted are you to your partner?			
How attractive do you feel around your partner?			
Total SEX LIFE Booms:			

YOUR BODY & HEALTH	BOOM	MEH	YUCK
How do you feel about your body right now?			
How do you feel when you look at yourself naked in the mirror?			
How do you feel about your current energy levels?			
How satisfied are you with your current health status?			
How satisfied are you with your current level of fitness?			
Do you believe you take excellent care of yourself?			
How would you rate your overall satisfaction with your physical state?			
Total BODY & HEALTH Booms:			

YOUR CREATIVE PURSUITS	BOOM	MEH	YUCK
Do you consider yourself a creative person?			
How do you feel about yourself as an artist?			
Do you have a creative outlet or hobby?			
How confident are you about your own creativity?			
How do you feel about your most recent creative project?			
How much fun do you have when you do creative stuff?			
How would you rate the amount of time you dedicate to creative pursuits?			
Total CREATIVITY Booms:			

YOUR ROMANTIC RELATIONSHIP(S)	BOOM	MEH	YUCK
If you're currently in a relationship, how do you feel about that relationship?			
If you're not currently in a relationship, how do you feel about the prospect of starting one?			
When you think about your romantic partner, how do you feel?			
When you think about the possibility of finding your ideal partner, how do you feel?			
What is your current level of satisfaction with your romantic partner (or the idea of finding one)?			
How satisfying is your current relationship?			
How do you feel this relationship (or pursuit of one) impacts you as an individual?			
Total RELATIONSHIP Booms:			

YOUR FRIENDS & SOCIAL CIRCLES	BOOM	MEH	YUCK
How satisfied are you with your social life?			
How expansive is your circle of friends?			
How do you feel around your friends?			
What is the overall impact of your friends and social groups on you as an individual?			
How close/connected do you feel to your friends?			
Do you feel as though you contribute to your friends and social groups?			
To what degree do you enjoy spending time with your friends and social relations?			
Total SOCIAL Booms:			

YOUR FAMILY	BOOM	MEH	YUCK
What is your current level of satisfaction with your family?			
How well do you get along with your family?			
How do you feel about yourself as a result of being around your family?			
How active and present are you when you're with your family?			
How much do you enjoy spending time with your family?			
Do you feel expansive (as though you become more) while around your family?			
What do you think is your overall impact on your family?			
Total FAMILY Booms:			

YOUR SPIRITUALITY	BOOM	MEH	YUCK
How spiritual do you consider yourself to be?			
How satisfied are you with your current level of spirituality?			
How good does your spirituality make you feel?			
To what degree are you able to enjoy and share your spirituality with others?			
What is the impact on you as an individual, as a result of your current level of spirituality?			
How do you feel about yourself as a result of your spirituality?			
How would you rate your overall happiness and satisfaction?			
Total SPIRITUALITY Booms:			

YOUR MENTAL STATE	BOOM	MEH	YUCK
Do you feel challenged and mentally stimulated?			
To what degree do you feel intelligent?			
What percentage of your time is spent stimulating yourself mentally?			
How do you feel about your mental growth?			
How satisfying is your mental achievement?			
Are you happy with your current level of mental stimulation?			
How would you compare your mental state with that of those around you?			
Total MENTAL Booms:			

Now add up the number of "Booms" you marked and enter the total for each category:

______ Your work life

______ Your sex life

______ Your body (and health)

______ Your creative pursuits

______ Your romantic relationship(s)

______ Your friends and social circles

______ Your family

______ Your spirituality

______ Your mental state

______ **Total Boom Score**

Math check: the highest possible score is between 63-72, depending on how many write-ins you added.

General Scoring Guidelines

0-10
Dangerously Low Boom Factor. Time to ratchet things up and seriously increase your Boom.

11-20
Low Boom. Review the list and look for which areas of your life need an immediate infusion of Boom.

21-30
Wimpy Boom. You may have one or two areas of life where things are smoking hot, but the rest aren't even smoldering. Your summary list will show you what areas could use a Boom infusion this year.

31-40

Moderate Boom. Some parts of life are really cranking, while others are fizzling. You likely already know what requires the most attention.

41-50

Excellent Levels of Boom. Life must feel pretty good to you right now. Scan the summary list for any numbers lower than 4 to see which areas may require special attention in the coming year.

51+

Outrageously High Boom. Are you feeling balanced and happy in life? If so, change nothing and focus on your goals for the year. But if you're feeling as though you've got too many plates spinning, it might be time to streamline and see which activities or responsibilities you might eliminate or scale back. Oooh *streamline!* That's the Boom word I chose for 2017. But we'll talk more about that when I help you choose *your* Boom word in Section 3.

★　★　★

Thanks to this exercise, you should now have a good grasp on what areas of your life are bringing you the greatest satisfaction, and which ones are in need of attention. Boom is a personal concept that is defined by you, so it's entirely up to you what you want to focus on improving for the coming year. Take a few minutes to make some notes about where in your life you'd like to infuse more Boom:

____

____

____

____

Completing the Past

Before we get too deep into what's next, it's important to look at what went right and what went not-so-fabulous in this past year. I've never been much of a history buff, and I hate to dwell on the past, but I find there is tremendous value in mentally completing the prior year before setting intentions for the next one. Think back to one year ago today and all that's happened (or hasn't happened) since.

What had you hoped to accomplish by now?

What achievements or "wins" can you celebrate from these past 12 months? HINT: I find it easier to review my calendar or day planner, rather than rely on my memory. But that's just me.

Where do you feel you fell short this past year?

Why didn't you accomplish these things? Be honest. See if you can take responsibility and ownership, without judgment.

____

____

____

____

____

What was your total income for the prior twelve months? How does this measure up against your expectations?

____

____

____

____

____

What ended in this past year? Your list might include specific relationships, careers, the life of a loved one or pet, ownership of a home or car, a long-term project or hobby, a debt you repaid, etc. Take some time to list everything that "completed" in the last year.

____

____

____

____

____

What began in this past year? Did you start a new job or career, develop a new relationship or friendship, pick up a new sport or hobby, or initiate a creative pursuit or project?

____

____

____

____

What lessons did you learn during these past 365 days?

____

____

____

____

How are you different now, as compared to this time last year? What changed about you? How have you grown?

____

____

____

____

____

What do you regret for the past year? How do you feel about that today?

____

____

____

____

If you could have one wish granted within the next twelve months, what would you wish for and why? What do you most want to shift or transform by the end of this coming year?

____

____

____

____

____

EXERCISE: Completing the Past

This is a visualization exercise I created for my private coaching clients when it's time to complete the past. I call it "Crossing the Line."

The concept is very simple. Imagine there is a line in the sand, which represents this moment, right now. Everything on one side of the line (the side you're currently standing on) represents your entire past, up until now.

To cross over the line is to leave the past in the past (where it belongs) and to step into a clean, clear future, where anything is possible. Once you cross the line, you do not look back over your shoulder. This is your way of filing the past stuff back where it belongs, in the dusty archives known as "stuff that happened."

Today, we'll use this exercise to complete the past year by crossing the line.

Once you step over the line, last year is complete and you are now moving forward into this new time period without being shackled by what did or didn't happen last year. Stepping across the line means giving yourself a clean slate and permission to be present in the now, in this new year.

I strongly recommend that when you are ready to complete this exercise, you close your eyes and vividly imagine the scene. Draw the line in the sand with your finger. Imagine wet sand that holds the line (as opposed to dry sand, that would fall back into place as your finger leaves).

Stand up and physically step over the line in whatever grand gesture feels most optimal to you as you play out this scene in your mind. Take a deep breath when you are done and when ready, open your eyes and turn the page to the next section.

This looks like a simple exercise, but don't underestimate its power. It only takes a minute and you'll be glad you did it.

See you on the other side....

Level 2: Crown

About the Crown Chakra

The crown chakra is located at the top of the head, toward the back, just over your crown. Jack fell down and broke his crown. Poor Jack, little did he know he had massive healing potential inside of himself, which could have rendered Jill's vinegar and brown paper unnecessary. But Jack, why did you attract such a fall in the first place?

Get Connected

The crown is our source of connectedness to God, Source, the Universe, All That Is, Ever Was, and Ever Shall Be. It is the seat of our spirituality, and the center of our bliss and beauty. The color most often associated with the crown chakra is violet or purple.

Like any effective planning session, we are beginning at the desired end result and working our way backward. We plan our work and work our plan, and that means starting with the end. Here, we begin with the crown and work our way down to the root chakra so that by the time you complete this workbook, you will have a clear and specific plan of action to take you from where you are now to where you want to be one year from now.

Now let's begin with **clarity** about what you really want.

Connecting to Source Energy

It is likely that you have a preferred name for what I am referring to here as "Source Energy." You might call it the Universe, God, Source, the Divine, the Greater Good, Mother Gaia, your Highest Self, Snookums, Yoda, Dumbledore, or any other label.

I am not particularly attached to any one name for this universal creative energy that connects and binds us. Therefore, I will stick to using the name "Source" or "Source Energy" and you can feel free to mentally substitute your preferred word for this phenomenon of ever-present creative energy.

We take a moment now to connect to Source Energy for the following reasons/benefits:

> Connecting will instantly center you and open you as a channel for what's possible.

> This process grounds you in the present moment, so that you can take a break from your to-do list and whatever else is on your mind at the moment.

> Clarity is easier to find when connected to Source.

> This process brings your energetic team into the foreground, which will help to grease the wheels for what's next.

> Connecting puts you in a space of what's possible as opposed to lower frequency questions such as "what do I need?" or "what should I want?"

> When you consciously open a channel to Source before doing anything, you will find that the whole energy around the task shifts for the better. I find this to be especially helpful when I am setting goals and intentions, as we will do here in this workbook.

> Besides which, opening your crown by connecting just feels good.

If you already have some experience connecting to Source, you can feel free to use your preferred method for this. Like eating a Reese's, there's no wrong way to do it. If it feels good and you feel expanded and calm, it's working.

Here are instructions in case you've never done this before:

Stand with your feet planted firmly on the ground, weight distributed evenly between both feet. Relax your knees. Close your eyes and relax. Relax your jaw, your shoulders, and your tongue.

Imagine there is a cord, any kind of cord or rope or string you like, running from the base of your spine all the way down to the center of the earth. This cord connects you, and you feel safe and grounded because of it. Now imagine that there is a funnel above your head, with the narrow part of the funnel leading down into your crown and the wide part of the funnel reaching up to the sky.

Now we're going to run some energy. Most people find this to be a very pleasant experience. Imagine that you are pulling energy up from the earth's core and allowing this energy to comfortably travel up your body, straight up in a line, and it moves all the way up and out through your crown. Now imagine that you are reaching high into the sky and pulling energy from the sky down through your funnel and into your crown. This energy travels down your body, down into your feet.

You can run this energy up and down your body as quickly or slowly as you like, as often as you wish, or you could stop here. When you feel relaxed, connected, energized, and expanded, it is complete.

Now that you are connected to Source energy, consider that anything is possible. Anything at all. Yes… even that.

With this divinely connected perspective that anything is possible for you, take some time to complete the following "If I could" statements. See if you can work through this exercise without judgment or critique. Simply write down your responses to each question, and if you find yourself beginning to erase, cross-out, or criticize, take a breath and say, "anything is possible" and then continue down the list. This exercise works best when your answers are quick and short, without a lot of thinking involved.

If I could have anything in the next twelve months, I would love to have (list as many as you wish):

____

____

____

____

____

____

____

____

____

If I could change one thing about myself, it would be:

____

____

If I could change one thing about my main relationship, it would be:

____

____

If I could change one thing about my career, it would be:

____

____

If I could change one thing about my finances, it would be:

____

____

If I could change one thing about my spiritual fulfillment or my relationship with Source, it would be:

____

____

If I could change JUST ONE thing about my body, it would be:

____

____

If I could change one thing about my home, it would be:

____

If I could change one thing about my life, it would be:

____

If I could get paid to do anything, I would love to get paid to:

____

____

If I could travel anywhere in the next 12 months, I would love to go to:

____

____

If I could meet anyone in the world, I would love to meet:

____

If I could attract all sorts of amazing people into my life, I would love to attract:

____

____

If I could do anything at all this year, I would love to:

____

____

In the realm of "anything is possible," I would love it if I could:

____

____

____

Now that you've opened your mind and expanded your thinking (anything is possible, right?), let's take a quick look at your relationship to Source.

Part of having a well-balanced, well-rounded life includes a solid foundation with Source Energy. If you're like most people, this is the relationship that tends to be the most fulfilling in your life, yet typically the one in which you invest the least amount of time and effort.

But this year doesn't have to be like that. You can now consciously create a strong, solid, loving, working (and playing) relationship with Source. If you choose to do this, you will be amazed at how beautifully and synchronistically the rest of your life unfolds!

Take a few minutes to answer these questions as honestly as possible. Remember, no one ever needs to see these answers except for you.

How would you describe your current relationship with Source?

____

____

____

If you could change anything about this relationship, what three things would you change and why?

____

____

____

____

How would your life transform as a result of changing the three things you listed above?

____

____

____

Take a moment to imagine your ideal relationship with Source Energy. Be as specific and detailed as possible in your visualization. Now describe it here:

____

____

____

____

____

____

What are the feelings you would experience as a result of having that ideal relationship with Source?

____

____

____

____

How would your life change for the better if you *now* had that ideal relationship with Source?

____

____

____

Sum up your desired end result (ideal relationship with Source) in three words or less and write it in the box below:

Are you satisfied with those three words? Do they fully and accurately capture the essence of what you'd love to create in this relationship? If so, please take a minute now to visually enhance the word(s). You might use a highlighter or a couple of markers to add some color, or you might take the space below to rewrite it and doodle some designs around the words, or you might reinforce the words so that they appear bolder or heavier in weight.

Ideally, we'd like these words to stand out in your mind as we move forward through the rest of this book, so whatever you do next, just make sure the words look appealing and carry some weight as you look at them.

Once you've completed that, you're ready to move on to the Third Eye section.

Level 3: Third Eye

About the Third Eye Chakra

The third eye chakra, sometimes called the third eye, is located in the middle of the forehead, between and just above the eyebrows. The band Third Eye Blind created the song "Jumper," which has arguably some of the finest song lyrics of our generation. If you're not familiar with it, trust me: just go buy the single from the iTunes store and you can thank me later. Dammit, now I've got that song stuck in my head.

Vision and Intuition

The third eye represents vision and intuition. It is the source of your imagination, wisdom, and clarity. The third eye is all about seeing the big picture and making decisions accordingly. The color most often associated with the third eye chakra is indigo or blue.

One of the questions people often ask me is "how can I open my third eye?" Here are two easy ways, almost too simple to be taken seriously. Almost. Because they seriously work.

The first is quick and painless. The second is a little freaky. You only need to do one to open your third eye right now, so make your choice based on how brave you're feeling.

Open Your Third Eye

The easiest way to open your third eye is to touch that spot on your forehead with your finger and say out loud or inside your head: "Please open my third eye." Then you can put your finger down and relax.

Some people will have an experience almost immediately, while others will shrug, assume nothing happened, and then later in the day they will have a profound third eye occurrence. This could appear as a moment of clarity or insight, or having a vision, or suddenly knowing the answer to a problem they've been struggling with for some time.

See? I did tell you it would almost be too simple to be taken seriously. (Almost.) Most people try to complicate the third eye or force a certain way of manifesting proof that it's open. Just ask for it to be open, and then relax and let inner vision unfold.

Now here's the freakier option, if you're feeling adventurous:

Stare at your reflection in a mirror. Keep your focus specifically on the area of your third eye. Settle in, because somewhere between a few and several minutes after you begin this, the image you see will change. It varies from person to person, but most people either see an eye at their third eye or they see a different face in place of their own. At which point, you freak out and shatter the illusion, and then you're back to looking your actual face, so you have to start from the beginning again to see anything cool. If you want to see multiple different faces, the trick is to stay calm and chill when your face changes and just keep staring at your third eye area.

Now that your third eye is open (as opposed to Third Eye Blind), it's time to begin to create your vision. We will begin this phase by prioritizing what you'd like to transform in the coming year.

Areas for Improvement

Take a few minutes now to identify seven areas (max) of your life you'd like to improve by this time next year. Review the previous exercises if necessary.

1.

2.

3.

4.

5.

6.

7.

Now **circle your top five.** Too tough? Use the process of elimination to deselect two choices as slightly lower priority than the rest. Once you've selected your top five, **put a star next to the top three.** Choose the three areas in your life have the potential to create the greatest overall impact on your happiness and well-being.

Now you have your top three priorities for transformation for the year. This doesn't mean you can't improve in all seven areas, but it's wise to narrow your focus. The mistake most people make when thinking about goals for a whole year is to create too many intentions. This diffuses your energy and mental focus, thereby producing less impactful results. Focusing your attention and energy on just three main areas will empower you to create clear and evident results, which brings greater satisfaction and achievement.

As you look at the top three priorities you've selected, **see if you can find a common theme.** For example, when I did this exercise way back in 2014, I knew I wanted to work fewer hours yet be more productive during work time, I wanted to spend more time with my family, and I wanted to increase my income. The common thread I found among these three was *leverage.*

If you're having trouble finding the common denominator of your top three priorities, use the mind mapping tool on the next page.

A **mind map** is a drawing or graphic designed to organize bits of information visually. Mind mapping works in conjunction with the natural processes of your brain to facilitate problem solving, brainstorm, get clarity, and organize your thoughts and ideas.

The Boom process works backwards. Normally, you would place the main topic in the center and then continue outwards from that point. However, since here we are mind mapping to discover the common theme, we'll leave the center blank and map the outer parts until it becomes clear what word or common theme belongs in the center.

On the "characteristic" lines, write the desired characteristics of each priority. For example, if you're working on your body, what are the characteristics of the results you wish to see? You might list words like fit, healthy, and sexy.

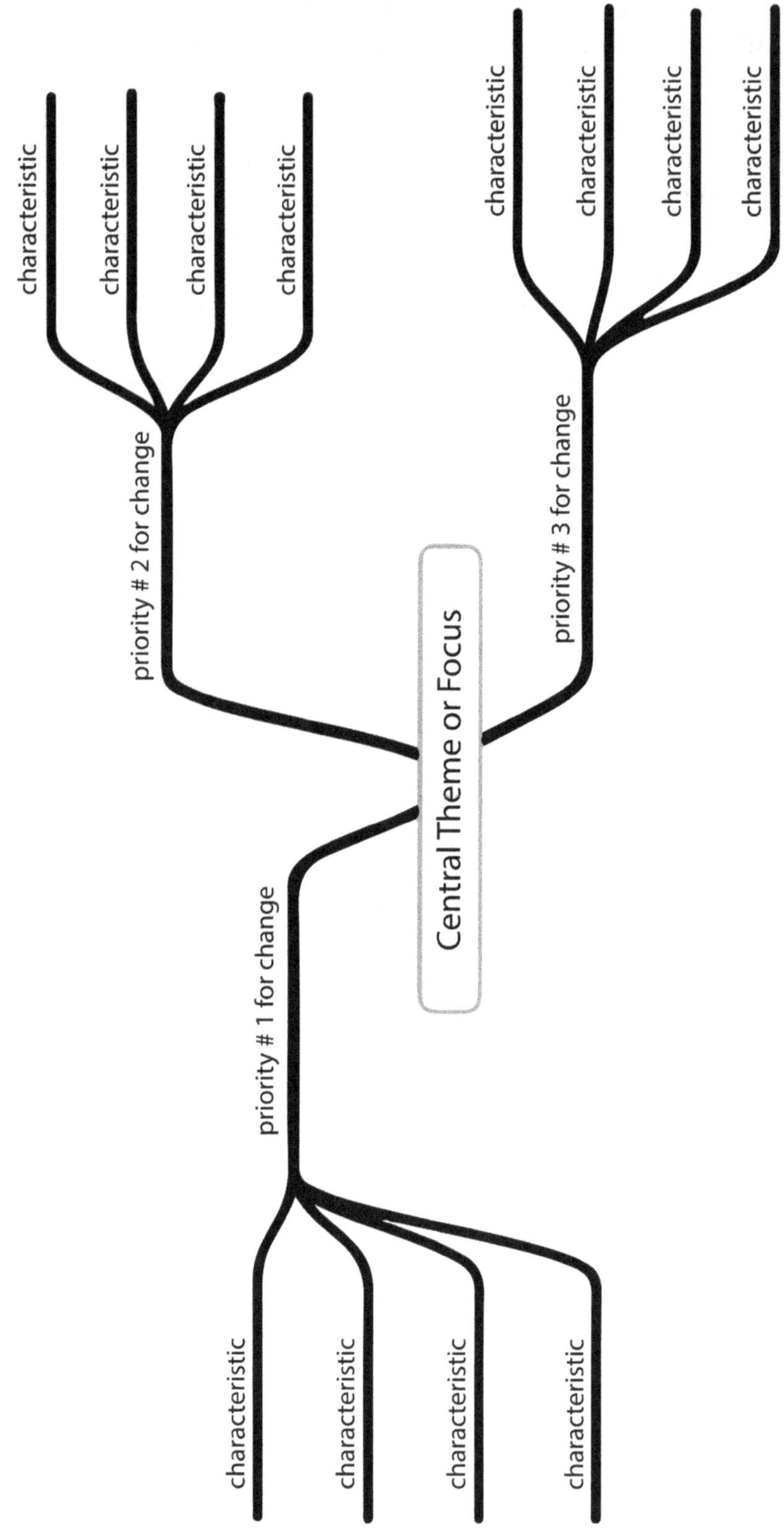

characteristic
characteristic
characteristic
characteristic
characteristic
characteristic
characteristic
characteristic
characteristic
characteristic
characteristic
characteristic
priority # 1 for change
priority # 2 for change
priority # 3 for change
Central Theme or Focus

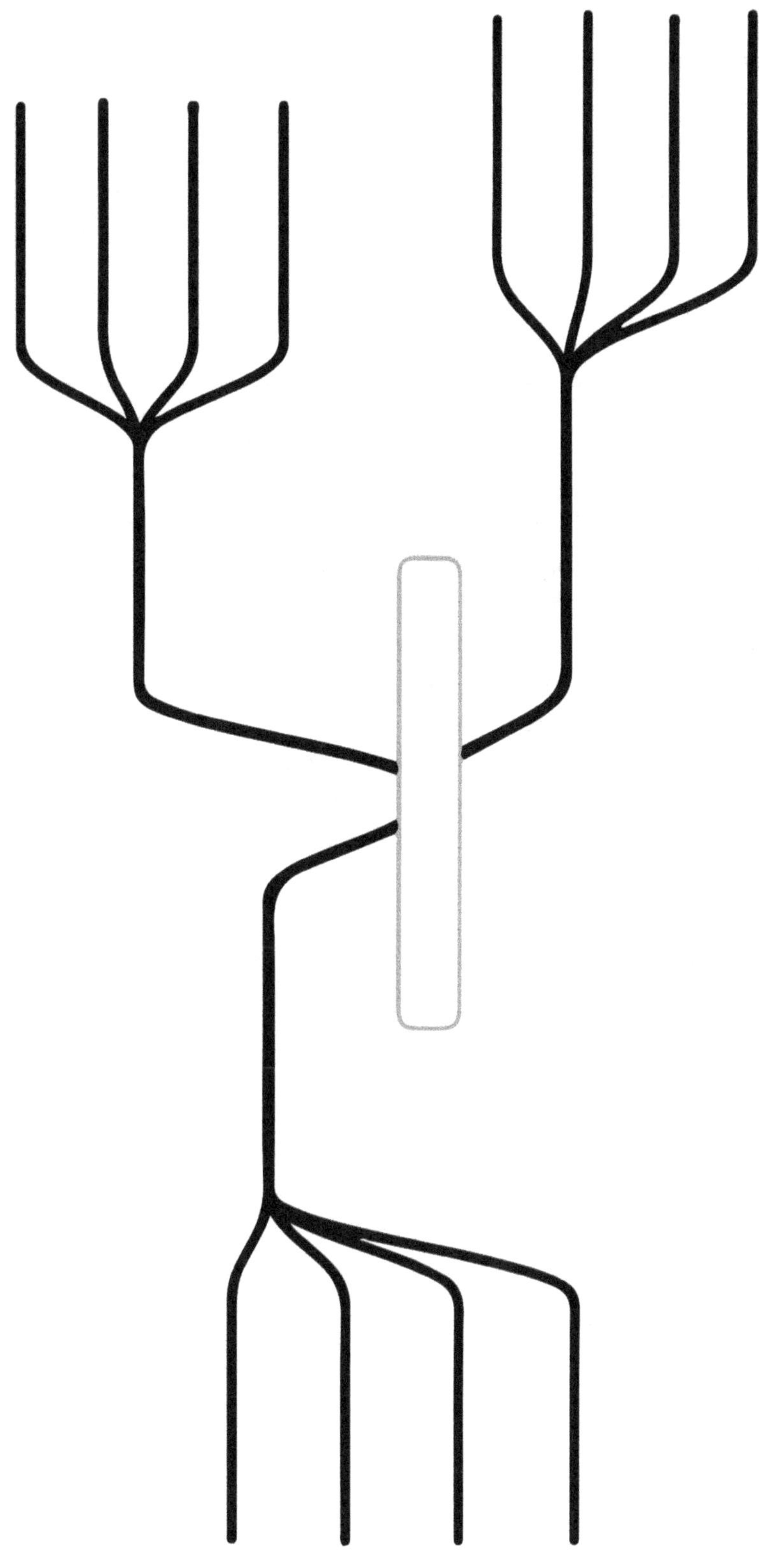

Add more lines to the mind map if you need to, but **once you've got the common thread that runs through all three priorities, write it here:**

____

Now look back at the rest of your list of seven areas for improvement. Does the common thread apply to any of the others? Most people find that their common thread runs through nearly their entire list. We will refer back to this common thread in a bit, so be sure to complete this before moving on.

Future Self Exercise

Essentially, you're going to look ahead at yourself, one year from now. You will reach out and connect to your future self. There are no wrong answers here, as your future self is determined by what you wish to create a year from now, and we've already begun to envision that. This is the next logical step in the process.

Answer the following questions from the perspective of your future self, one year from today. Imagine you have a time machine, and you travel forward in time by one year to find that you've successfully achieved your goals. What would your present self like to ask your future self? The questions below are designed to get you started, but you can begin a dialogue with your future self during which you can ask anything you like. You can use the "I" or "we" version of each question, depending on which feels better or makes more sense to you.

This exercise is key in the strategic planning process, so that your brain begins to work backward from a point of future success, and it will help you determine (consciously or subconsciously) which problems need to be solved in what manner, and which steps are necessary in order to create the desired end result.

What is today's date? _______________________________________

(HINT: the answer from your future self will be exactly one year from today. Answer all questions as though you are looking back from the point of view of this future date.)

What was the single best thing I (we) created this past year?

____

____

____

How am I (are we) different now as compared to a year ago?

____

____

____

What did I (we) learn?

____

____

____

What finally got resolved this year?

____

____

____

What was my (our) biggest accomplishment?

____

____

How do I (we) feel now that I've (we've) achieved that accomplishment?

____

____

____

What kinds of words of encouragement or congratulations did other people say to me (us) when I (we) achieved it? What specifically did they say?

____

____

____

What's next for me (us)?

____

____

____

Take this space to continue the dialogue and to ask your future self anything you wish.

____

____

____

____

____

____

____

____

Have you ever created a **one hundred list?** Remember I mentioned that people who write down their goals are approximately ten times more likely to achieve those goals than a person who does not write them down? Well, you might be surprised to learn that the success rate is also high for people who simply *draft a list of desires.*

This is similar to a "bucket list" but instead of writing down things you want to do before you kick the bucket, you'll write a list of things you want to do in the next 365 days. I normally make my list in January, so I'm thinking of what I want to have, do, or be before celebrating the next New Year's Eve. For that reason, I call it "The Fireworks 100."

Will you actually do *everything* on your list? Uncommon, but not impossible. Regardless, here are some of the benefits of creating a Fireworks 100 list:

> Opens your creative channels as you push to think of more than twenty things

> Helps you focus on what you want

> Brings clarity around what you're creating this year

> Cultivates a brainstorming effect: the onset of ideas brings forth new and unexpected ideas

> Engages that powerful brain of yours to find ways to manifest what you've set forth on paper

> Keeps you in the realm of "anything is possible"

> Nudges you beyond your comfort zone

> Items on your list will manifest in strange and delightfully unexpected ways, sometimes differently than you imagined, and sometimes at the very last minute.

In 2015, one of the things I put on my Fireworks 100 list was "help a young entrepreneur get started in business." At the time, I was thinking I would provide seed money to a young person with a great idea, or perhaps offer some free business advice. What actually manifested that year was a business for my eldest daughter, who was just ten years old at the time. I provided business advice and helped her to get started with her first clients. If you're curious, you can see her business here:

http://custompendulums.com

Never, ever give up

It is not uncommon for items on your Fireworks 100 list to come to fruition after you've given up on them or forgotten them entirely, sometimes at the eleventh hour.

In 2014, I wrote on my Fireworks 100 that I wanted to meet Frank Kern in person and attend one of his live events. I loved working with Frank as part of his Mastermind Alliance during the previous year, and I thought it would be cool to hang with him in person. By November, I had given up on that one, since I didn't see any possibility of it happening, and the end of the year is always so busy for me.

Then, just weeks before the close of the year, I got a surprise personal invite to attend Frank's three-day workshop in San Diego. It just so happened to jive with my schedule, so I went. I had a blast and learned a ton. Did I mention I was invited to attend as his guest? That's right, I manifested an $8000 ticket to that event, *for free*. It all started because I wrote it on my Fireworks 100 list, and it ultimately manifested at the eleventh hour, just three weeks before the year-end fireworks.

There are countless stories about goals coming into reality at the eleventh hour. Adjust your strategy, yes, but never give up.

As you fill in the next couple of pages for your Fireworks 100, remember… anything is possible!

1.	21.
2.	22.
3.	23.
4.	24.
5.	25.
6.	26.
7.	27.
8.	28.
9.	29.
10.	30.
11.	31.
12.	32.
13.	33.
14.	34.
15.	35.
16.	36.
17.	37.
18.	38.
19.	39.
20.	40.

41.   63.

42.   64.

43.   65.

44.   66.

45.   67.

46.   68.

47.   69.

48.   70.

49.   71.

50.   72.

51.   73.

52.   74.

53.   75.

54.   76.

55.   77.

56.   78.

57.   79.

58.   80.

59.   81.

60.   82.

61.   83.

62.   84.

85.   93.

86.   94.

87.   95.

88.   96.

89.   97.

90.   98.

91.   99.

92.   100.

Your BOOM Word

I mentioned earlier that the common thread for my top three areas for improvement a couple years ago was "leverage," which actually became my **Boom word** for 2014.

Creating a single word focus is powerful for a number of reasons:

> ➤ Helps you channel your energy and your mental vision, adding power and concentration to focus your efforts.

> ➤ Spills over into all areas of your life. I intended to leverage my work efforts, but ultimately, I created leverage of personal responsibilities, finances, net worth, family time, and my health.

> ➤ Alleviates pressure by giving you just one thing to focus on for the year.

> ➤ Guides your business and personal decisions.

> ➤ Gives you a benchmark for making tough decisions and measuring progress. Simply ask: Will this move me closer to (insert your word) or farther away from it? Suddenly, the choice becomes clear.

It is possible to have a different Boom word for your personal life and for business. But in most cases, you can find a single powerful word to fit both.

Your Boom word for the year may or may not be the same as the common thread you identified earlier in this section.

Here's how to know if you've selected your most optimal focus for this year:

> Getting this one thing will make a huge difference in your life.

> Achievement of this word brings impact. Big impact.

> When you say (or think) the word, you feel inspired and uplifted.

> The word resonates as a strong YES throughout your body.

> Saying the word out loud feels delicious, through and through.

The word may take anywhere from a few minutes to several days to decide. In 2015, it took me a long while to come up with "elevate." Every word I considered felt close, but not quite right. But my Boom word for 2017 ("streamline") popped in out of nowhere, two months before I started working in that year's Boom book.

Here I will strongly encourage you to **take your time** and really get the right word. Once you find a word that resonates, look up its actual definition. The dictionary definition of a word carries weight energetically, so be sure to choose a word with a clear meaning that strongly resonates with what you want to achieve in this coming year.

If you get stuck or you find a word that's close but no cigar, check out *thesaurus.com* for some ideas and words with similar meanings. Set the intention that the right word will come to you, and that you'll know it when it arrives. When it does, write it down here:

My **Boom** word for the year is:

Now that you've got your Boom word, why not pop on over to Club Clarity and let us all know what you picked? Be sure to mention you heard about it here in the Boom book!

Facebook.com/groups/askamyanything

Level 4: Throat

About the Throat Chakra

You guessed it, this chakra is located at the throat, and it is the center for communication and transformation. This is the area that locks up and shuts down when you refrain from speaking your truth. But when it's open and spinning freely, manifestation flows more quickly and readily.

The throat is the chakra for truth and self-expression. The color associated with the throat chakra is light blue.

First, tell the truth

Before we can create any kind of shift or transformation, we must first **tell the truth about what's so, right now.** It's like they say: the first step toward solving a problem is admitting you have one. It's no wonder so many thyroid problems are related to underlying issues around not speaking one's truth.

These next exercises are designed to help you tell the truth about the current status in your life. We're not going to dwell on what's wrong; we are simply going to tell the truth about what's what, so that you can see where you are starting from, right here, right now. Got it? Here we go.

Telling the Truth

Remember in Level 3 where you set your top seven priorities for improvement, and then we narrowed it down to five, and then three? Turn back to that page and just below each one, give a one- or two-sentence summary of the current status quo.

Here are a couple of examples to help you get started:

1. *Relationship w/partner.*
We love each other, but there's never enough time, not
enough sex, intimacy, or romance. We haven't made our

relationship a priority for years, and neither of us seems to know how to fix it.

2. My business.

Business is good, but growth has been flat for more than a year now. Want to take it to the next level, but that's exhausting to even think about and I'm not sure I'm up for it or that I even know how.

Get the picture? Just write a couple of sentences that honestly and objectively tell the truth about these areas you want to improve. Interestingly enough, if you are completely truthful in this exercise, you will likely write things that have been circling the back of your mind, but that you never dared to admit, write, or say out loud. That's exactly what creates blockages in the throat chakra. This is your opportunity to tell the truth.

Amazing things happen when we tell the truth. The most immediate benefit is that you no longer have to expend mass quantities of energy and effort concealing the truth, fabricating partially believable justifications and rationalizations, judging yourself for thinking it, or trying not to think about it.

Try telling the truth now and see for yourself what happens. I promise you will feel better.

Tell the truth and feel better fast

Over the next couple of weeks, notice when your throat feels tight or closed. Tell the truth about something, which could be as simple as responding "maybe not your best look" instead of "nah, you look great" when your girlfriend asks if these jeans make her butt look big. Then notice the difference in how your throat feels.

Whew. Okay, the hard part is over. Next, we'll use the following series of questions to further clarify what you'd like to create and attract in the coming year. Once you complete this next exercise, I bet you'll find at least a few more items to add to your Fireworks 100 list, if you haven't already filled it up.

Unlike the prior set of questions where you were asked to write the first thing that popped into your head, I'm inviting you to think a minute or two about these answers.

What kind of people do you want to attract into your life this year?

\
\
\

What relationships need to terminate this year?

\
\

Which relationships deserve to be transformed this year?

\
\

What changes would you love to see in your family this year?

\
\
\

What specific places would you love to visit (can be local or otherwise)?

\
\
\

What kinds of shows would you love to see this year? (Comedy, theater, concerts, ballet, symphony, art, sports, crafts, monster trucks, etc.)

____

____

____

If you could have a creative "play date" with yourself, what kinds of things would you like to do?

____

____

____

What kind of romantic dates would you like to go on this year?

____

____

What would you like to create (art, jewelry, a book or short story, etc.)?

____

____

____

What new foods or cuisines do you want to try this year?

____

____

____

What have you *not* done in a really long time that you'd like to do again this year?

____

____

How would you like to enhance your home?

____

____

____

How much money would you like to make this year?

____

What changes would you like to see in your career in the coming year?

____

____

What kind of help would you love to attract into your career or business this year?

____

____

What sorts of charitable contributions, donations, or volunteer work would you like to give this year?

____

____

____

How would you love to transform your body?

____

____

What specific changes would you love to see in your health over the next twelve months?

____

____

Which habits would you love to break?

____

____

What new habits would you like to establish?

____

____

____

How would you like to enhance your romantic relationship?

____

____

What changes would you love to see in your main relationship this year?

____

____

What needs to "complete" this year so that you can move on?

____

____

____

How would you love to stimulate and challenge your mind this year?

____

____

What kind of spiritual retreat or reflection do you want to create this year?

____

____

What would be the most satisfying outcome for you for the year, spiritually speaking?

____

____

Anything else you'd like to add or create for the upcoming year?

____

____

____

____

____

It is likely that while you were answering the last set of questions, some of the answers you wrote may have felt far-fetched or even impossible to you. This next exercise can help with that.

According to the late Louise Hay (author of countless books, perhaps best known for *You Can Heal Your Life* and the creation of Hay House Publishing), you don't have to know how to change; you just have to be willing to change. Our pal Louise recommended this quick and simple transformation process for activating that all-important throat chakra:

To Activate the Throat Chakra:

Touch your throat lightly and say out loud, "I am willing, I am willing, I am willing."

You can use this as part of a specific statement, as in: "I am willing to forgive so-and-so," or "I am willing to receive my soul mate," or "I am willing to consider hiring an assistant," or you can just use the "I am willing" statement by itself.

If you find you have resistance to the statement, you can take it one step further and say, "I am willing to be willing to…" or even just "I am willing to be willing."

Read back through your answers from the previous exercise and look for any answers you wrote that seem far-fetched. For each one, use the "I am willing" statement three times, combined with a light touch of your throat. Now you are on your way.

Language Police

If you find yourself using words like "want" or "need," which are low-frequency words that operate at lower vibrations, here is a simple way to transform that and to elevate your vibe. Switch to phrases like "I require" or "I would love" or "I deserve" or "I now receive" in place of "I want" and "I need."

Try saying the following statements out loud and notice how the language feels to you.

I need to go to the store and get milk.

I want to meet the man of my dreams.

I gotta find a new job.

Now try these:

> *I require some fresh milk.*
>
> *I would love to meet the man of my dreams, so bring him on.*
>
> *I am so ready for an awesome job close to my home, with fabulous pay and wonderful people.*

The essence is the same, and yet it's the framing of the language that makes all the difference. Words like *choose, receive, now, allow, love, deserve, ready for,* and *accept* carry a much higher vibration than words that inherently imply lack.

Begin to incorporate these higher vibration words and statements when expressing what you want and need in your life. Consider that every time you open your mouth, you're creating something, so why not create more of what you want instead of what you don't want?

Level 5: Heart and Soul

Congratulations! You have reached a pivotal point in this workbook. This is the point where we shift from the head—thinking, visioning, and imagining—into the body. Action does it and we're now going to move into the action part of this process.

The Heart Chakra

The heart chakra is not located in your heart organ; rather, it's in the middle of your chest, between and slightly above the breasts. Top o' the cleavage, ma'am.

As expected, the heart chakra is all about giving and receiving love. But you might be surprised to learn this center is also the source of joy, peace, and being open to receive love, money, opportunity, and a whole lot more. A closed heart chakra will make it difficult to freely receive cash, acknowledgment, opportunities, and countless other blessings.

Opening the heart chakra ensures that you are open to receive what you desire most, including material and non-material gifts. The color most often associated with the heart chakra isn't pink, but *green*.

The Opening

Before we dive into action, I am going to lead you through an opening. I use the term "opening" to describe an energetic process that opens you up or expands your awareness in some way. Remember when I taught you how to open your third eye? Yup, that was an opening.

Without this step, the actualization is slow and plodding, or results may not manifest at all. Preparing yourself to receive will ensure that things can happen as quickly as you are willing to allow them.

For some people, heart chakra work brings feelings of vulnerability or exposure. I'm going to show you a simple opening exercise, which most people find to be pleasant and enjoyable. If for some reason you find it to be scary or unpleasant, that's a good indication that your heart chakra is significantly blocked, and clearing is warranted. If you'd like my help in clearing this, you can either grab a copy of my book *1-2-3 Clarity!* or reach out to me for assistance (see the last few pages of this book to find out how).

Have you ever seen a time-lapse photography video? A long, slow process is recorded, and then played back at a much faster speed. When I was a kid, I remember watching PBS television and seeing a seedling turn into a sprout and then into a plant. It was fascinating. In just a minute or two, the time-lapse video revealed a process that normally takes a month or more to occur in nature. Okay, keep that image in mind as we move into this opening.

Even though green is the color most frequently associated with the heart chakra, we will work with soft pink for this opening, because it is the color of unconditional love. Remember, the heart chakra is at the center of your chest at the top o' the cleavage. Let's begin.

> *First, take a few moments to get comfortable and relax. Focus on your breathing, in and out. Turn your attention to your heart chakra, at the center of your chest. As you relax, consider your intention for this opening. Your intention is to open yourself up to receive your good. Whatever you desire is fine, whether it's more love, money, gifts, friendship, clients, intimacy, recognition, acknowledgement, success, opportunities, travel, time off, creativity, or anything else you wish.*

> *Feeling nice and relaxed? Good. Next we are going to imagine a soft pink rosebud, not yet in bloom. This tight little bud is located at your heart chakra. Now, in time-lapse video fashion, imagine that the little rosebud is opening up wide, wide, wide, into a large and beautiful flower. This is the most gorgeous pink rose you have ever seen, and it's here at your heart chakra. Breathe deeply as you roll your shoulders back to further open up the chest. Notice how you feel.*

This opening typically instills feelings of peace, tranquility, readiness, and relaxation, and you may be experiencing these now. If you wish, you can create an "I am open" statement or two, to sustain this newfound sense of openness. Here are a few examples to get you started:

I am open to receive my good.

I am open to receive more ___________________.

I am open to all good things.

I am now open and ready to receive.

I am open to _______________________________.

Calendar Your Results

Now that you are open and ready to receive, the next step is to make some space in your life. The first way to do this is by **calendaring your results.** This is a simple process that makes a world of difference in dreaming about something versus actually achieving specific results within a specific time frame.

Grab a highlighter and your calendar or day planner or smartphone. I'll just go get myself a coconut water while you do that. Meet you back here in five.

With your highlighter in hand, flip back through this book. Beginning with the "Anything Is Possible" exercise in the crown chakra section, highlight any desire you wrote that meets **both** of the following criteria:

> ➤ **You still want to create it**

> ➤ **It is specific and can be attached to a certain date.**

For example, "feel better about myself" would not qualify because it's not specific, yet "travel to Barcelona" would. Anything that feels "meh" at this point can be skipped over. Sometimes we get caught up in the moment while writing, or we write things we think we should want, which aren't actually inspiring enough to sustain us through any substantial action.

Include items in your Fireworks 100 while highlighting. You may even think of more to add to your 100 list as you go through this part. Happy highlighting! I'll just be here, sipping my coconut water and checking email. Meet you back here in twenty.

Excellent! Now we can move on. Full disclosure: this next step takes a while, usually a long while (depending on how many items you highlighted). However, it is totally worth it because it is key in ensuring you actually achieve what you want.

Go into your calendar and schedule in everything you highlighted. Right now, we're just calendaring simple reminders and end results, not the specific action steps or milestones it will take to get there. Here are a few examples for your reference:

If your highlighted desires included:

> ➤ Weekly date nights with my sweetie

> ➤ Travel to Barcelona

> ➤ Attend a spiritual retreat

Then you could calendar these results in this way:

- ➢ Create a recurring reminder every Sunday afternoon from now until a year from now: Discuss and plan this week's date night with sweetie

- ➢ January 15 reminder: begin planning trip to Barcelona

- ➢ February 1 reminder: look into spiritual retreats (HINT: ask Amy Scott Grant about her next retreat. These life-changing events are not publicized and are by invitation only.)

Git 'er done

Calendaring these events into your digital schedule or physical day planner helps ensure you'll take the necessary steps to create results. Plus, if it's in your calendar, you can't say you don't have time. #sorry #notsorry

If you're anything like me, your natural instinct would be to create a mile-long laundry list of things to do on the first of next month, but resist that urge and try to spread things out a bit. That way, you'll avoid overwhelm and actually make forward progress instead of chucking it all and biting your nails like crazy from the stress. Another easy way to prime the pump of receiving is to make space, literally.

Clearing Clutter

Clearing out the crap releases stagnant energy and allows things to move more freely in your life. It's like saying "yes" to what you want by getting rid of what you don't want. Additionally, it frees up space in your brain and creates an opening for good things to arrive. Every time I clean out a drawer or closet, money shows up. Sometimes it happens while I'm cleaning, when I find a forgotten check or a twenty-dollar bill. Other times, unexpected sales or funds appear almost immediately afterward. I can't tell you how many times a new client or student has enrolled while I was buried in my closet or basement or garage, busy with sorting and organizing and disposing of things. Now that's what I call *Boom*.

I can almost hear you saying, "I know, I get all that, but who has the time? I'll never get that closet/garage/basement/attic cleaned out." I hear you, but it's easier than you think. The trick is to break it down into smaller, more manageable chunks. Instead of thinking about tackling the entire room, why not address one quadrant of the room at a time?

If you're working on something that can't be broken down spatially, then use **time** as the breakdown factor. Set a timer for thirty minutes, and work diligently and in a focused fashion until the timer goes off. Don't answer your phone or check email during that time. Don't play with the stuff you've newly found. Just sort and organize and pitch whatever you can. **It's amazing what you can accomplish in a half hour when you've eliminated all distractions.**

Once you hear that timer go off, you can walk away without guilt or remorse. Most people find they want to reset the timer and do another thirty minutes, and while thirty minutes may not sound like much to you, you'd be amazed how quickly your efforts add up.

I once had a client who had piled up six months' worth of business paperwork. She normally filed monthly, which was very manageable, but life got in the way and next thing she knew, her desk was covered with half a year's paper trail. At that point, the task felt overwhelming and too big to tackle. But every time she sat at her desk, the towering pile of papers loomed over her like a black cloud. I asked her how long she estimated it would take if she were to work straight through. She guessed about six hours. Ugh! No wonder it felt overwhelming! When was the last time you had six hours to kill in one day? And if you did, you sure as hell didn't want to spend it filing papers!

I advised her to use the timer method I described to you above. We also set a deadline for completion, based on how much time she estimated she could devote to the task. She decided she would set her timer for forty minutes at a time, and she would complete the task within four weeks. Considering it had taken six months to pile up, one month seemed reasonable to un-pile it.

As it turned out, she found enthusiasm once she began the task, and completed it all within four days. That's less than a week! The entire task only took her *four hours*. She averaged an hour a day for four days, and then six months of feeling "ugh, I'll never get around to that" was forever erased from her brain. Can you imagine how much lighter she felt once it was done?

It takes a great deal of energy to maintain resistance and **not** do something. Once you stop resisting, you get immediate relief, like easing out of high heels after a long day of standing and walking. Here's what you can do with all that stuff you're purging:

Donate it ★ Sell it ★ Gift it ★ Recycle it ★ If nothing else applies, then Trash it

What is one icky space you've wanted to clean up, but haven't made the time for? Just name one that you're willing to tackle this coming year:

What is one small space (could be a drawer or under a bed) that you will commit to cleaning out *this week,* with the intention to prime the pump of receiving?

Take a minute now to schedule time into your calendar for cleaning that small space this week. You can do it!

The third way to create more space in your life is by performing clearing work. If you're not already familiar with my processes for clearing, you can start with the tools in my book, *1-2-3 Clarity! Banish Your Blocks, Doubts, Fears, and Limiting Beliefs Like a Spiritual Badass.*

Level 6: Solar Plexus

About the Solar Plexus Chakra

The **solar plexus** is a complex and dense network (plexus) of nerves that radiates outward like the sun's rays, from just behind the stomach. Think of it as a busy relay station for your nerves.

The **solar plexus chakra** is located just below the sternum, where your ribs attach in the front. Energetically speaking, this is where you hold your sense of self. This chakra is partly related to your identity (who you know yourself to be), but it is also closely aligned with self-love, self-image, confidence, power, and control. The color most often associated with the solar plexus chakra is yellow.

Are you familiar with Human Design? Essentially, it is a system for understanding your individual potential. Human Design synthesizes astrology, the I Ching, the chakra system, and the Kabbalah. Personally, I like it because it is hands down the most accurate charting system I have ever encountered. If you'd like to know all about *your* Human Design, visit my website for the hookup: **http://AskAmyAnything.com/humandesign**

Now let's explore how Human Design plays into our work here with the solar plexus.

Defined vs. Undefined Sense of Self

If you know a bit about Human Design, you may already be aware that your solar plexus can either be *defined* or *undefined*. There are pros and cons to both, and it's best to make the most of whatever you've got, rather than trying to adapt to be what you're not. If that concept sounds familiar, it's because it's the basic premise of any self-love work: love thyself, as is.

A *defined* solar plexus means you know who you are, and you are always that person, no matter where you are or whom you're with. The upside of having a defined solar plexus is that you are more prone to confidence and consistency, as you are always the same person with the same sense of self and the same ideals.

The downside of this is that others may find you to be rigid and unwavering in your ideals and values. People may make snap decisions and decide instantly whether or not they like you, and whether or not they deem you to be "one of them." Another upside is that you probably won't care too much if they don't accept you, because you never really felt at home with them in the first place.

An *undefined* solar plexus means you have an unformed sense of self. You tend to take on the identity or characteristics of those around you. The downside to this is that whenever you are not part of a group or community, or if you find yourself between relationships, you may feel like a ship adrift at sea. The upside is that you blend well with groups, fitting in almost instantly. You find yourself easily able to adapt to the norms and the cultures of a group, and groups will likely welcome you with open arms. Another downside is the possibility that you may unknowingly join a cult, but the upside to that is you won't see it as a cult while you're a part of it. Perhaps ignorance is bliss, after all.

Based on the explanation of what it means to have a defined or undefined solar plexus, which do you think best describes you and why?

Solar Plexus Strategy

Here are some factors to consider, based on whether your sense of self is defined or undefined.

Strategy for Defined Sense of Self: Part of your strategy for this year will be to harness your inherent sense of purpose and direction. This personal almanac is helping you to define and describe your goals and priorities for the year, and it will be up to you (you fabulous, authentic self, you) to spearhead those efforts. This may mean that you need to spend some time developing your ability to lead and direct, as well as your confidence to do so.

Strategy for Undefined Sense of Self: Are you currently a part of a group or community? If not, you may feel as though you are wandering a bit. Take some time to think about and jot down what kind of people you'd love to surround yourself with. Create a powerful intention for attracting your ideal community to show up for you, and know that they are lucky to have you! Commit to yourself to accept nothing less than the most optimal invitations that lead you closer to your desired result.

Shared Strategy for Both Types (Defined and Undefined): If you are currently a part of a group that no longer resonates with your new priorities for this year, now is the time to break your association. To channel a clear and direct focus is to ensure that all aspects of your life are in alignment. Like I always say: "If it ain't congruent, don't do it."

Same goes for toxic relationships. Rip off those band aids, babe. Set the energy vampires free and don't worry; they'll find a new host victim soon enough.

If you have an undefined sense of self and you're currently in a relationship (any kind of relationship) that's not working anymore, I would recommend that you find and settle into a community *before* you sever the relationship. Otherwise, you may find yourself untethered or ungrounded. Transition into a group, and then release the relationships that need to go.

Whether you have a defined or undefined sense of self, take a few minutes now to calendar any reminders or actions that support you in the strategies you identified above.

★ ★ ★

Introverts and Extroverts

Many people mistakenly believe that an extrovert is a "people person" and an introvert is someone who is shy or guarded. But in actuality, the distinction between the two rests in where you feel most energized. Being a people person doesn't automatically make you an extrovert.

My sister is one of the most outgoing and friendly people you'll ever meet. She's a flight attendant, and before that, she worked for years in the hotel-restaurant tourism industry. But she also needs her down time alone, to recharge her batteries. As much as she loves to be around people, if she spends too much time around others, she feels drained and wiped out. Alone time energizes her and allows her to be Miss Personality whenever she's around people. You'll walk away feeling amazing after an interaction with my sister, but if you stop to think about what was actually said in the conversation, you'll likely realize that she guided the conversation to be all about you, and you are left knowing very little about her. She talks very little about herself. All of this is what makes her an introvert.

How about you? If you go to a party or social gathering, how do you feel when it's time to go? Are you disappointed that the party is breaking up, feeling you could have continued for hours more? Or are you secretly glad for the break, so that you can go home and enjoy some peace and quiet in your jammies?

Conversely, how do you feel when you spend time alone? Do you ever travel or go to the movies alone? When you've been alone for a long while, how do you feel afterwards? Are you rested and renewed, or are you listless, wanting to get out and be social?

Introvert or Extrovert?

Being introverted or extroverted isn't absolute; it's more of a continuum, and most people have tendencies toward one side more than the other. We all have characteristics of both, but usually one is more predominant for you.

When someone asks you a question or invites you to do something, do you usually respond immediately (extrovert) or do you need several seconds to think about it (introvert)?

If you're scratching your head now because you could swear you are fully both, then you might be like me. I am very much in the middle of the introvert/extrovert spectrum. My best strategy is to strive for balance between the two. If I don't spend enough time alone, I feel scattered and unfocused. If I spend too much time alone, I wax cynical, forget to shower, and get stinky. When I'm out of balance, I get crabby until I put things back into alignment.

When people come to visit me, I'm delighted to have them, and I'm delighted when they leave. For me, that illustrates my need for balance. Now it's your turn.

As an (introvert or extrovert) ____________________, I can ensure that I remain balanced and get what I need by remembering to do the following:

____

____

____

____

____

____

Whether you are an introvert or extrovert (or both), take a few minutes now to **calendar the activities** that will support you in maintaining balance.

Self-Love

The first time I finished the following statement was a major turning point in my life. My hope is that it does the same for you. My answers have changed over the years, and yours likely will as well. When you read the question, just go with the first thing that pops into your head, no matter how strange or silly it might sound to you. Your first instinct here will be the most telling.

If I really loved myself, I would ____.

Release any judgment you have around your answer. For some, this is an emotional question that brings tears or sadness. My first answer all those years ago was "get a massage every week." I scoffed at that answer. It seemed too simple to me, too trivial. I wanted to answer with something more profound or substantial. But I wrote it down anyway and marveled at the fact that I had only allowed myself to have a massage on rare occasions, even though I could afford regular massages. Despite the fact that at that time, I couldn't quite imagine getting a massage every week (which felt incredibly lavish and indulgent to me then) I made a decision to learn to love myself more. Then the most amazing thing happened.

Within just a couple of weeks, a friend introduced me to a massage therapist who asked me for a trade. Trading healing sessions with me for massages with her eliminated my need to justify the cost of a weekly massage. That proved to me that my own level of self-love was on the rise. We cannot underestimate the power of self-love and its impact on our lives. Even for something as simple as a massage.

What would you do, have, or be, if you really loved yourself? Take some time to think about your answer. Is it possible, yet you won't allow yourself to have it? Or does it seem impossible to you? What are your thoughts and feelings about your answer?

____

____

____

____

What would it take for you to show yourself more love and kindness?

____

____

____

What can you do _today_ to love yourself more?

____

____

____

Besides self-love, the solar plexus is also the home of your **identity,** or who you know yourself to be.

Can you think of at least one way it seems you always _have_ to be, no matter what, as if you can't help yourself?

For example, try saying the words "I AM" before each of the following words, and circle the ones that feel as though they resonate for you:

Competitive	**Smart**	**Leader**
Proud	**Ridiculous**	**Shy**
Inappropriate	**Slow**	**Careless**
Strong	**Scared**	**Weak**
Polite	**Funny**	**Brave**
Attractive	**Loud**	**Insignificant**

Identity statements define more than a characteristic or personality trait. They are pervasive, woven into the very fabric of your being. Once you identify them, you start to notice these core beliefs in everything you say and do.

An identity statement often begins with the words "I am" and is typically very short. Whenever I do identity work with people, they try to qualify their identity statements (for example, "I am usually patient in difficult situations" as opposed to simply: "I am patient"). An identity statement is like a principle or a value: it's short, simple, and absolute. It may even appear oversimplified to you. Identity statements do not include the word "not."

If you're having trouble coming up with your own identity statements, think about what people often compliment you for, or what your parents or teachers frequently asked you to stop doing.

Identity statements

> ➤ Begin with "I AM"
> ➤ Are very short, usually three to five words.
> ➤ May appear over-simplified.
> ➤ Are true throughout all facets of your life and self.

Here are a few examples that demonstrate how to transform a statement with qualifiers into a true identity statement:

I am always getting in people's way. ➔ I am a nuisance.

I am a person who likes to be in charge. ➔ I am a leader.

I am emotionally strong. ➔ I am strong.

I am not creative. ➔ "Not" is not part of an identity statement, so ask: what am I? You might find an answer like: I am a follower. I am a good girl. I am obedient. I am kind. I am blank. I am unoriginal. I am orderly. Get the picture?

Take a few minutes now to think about and jot down some of your existing identity statements. I've purposely kept the lines below short, so you won't be tempted to qualify. Just keep the statements short and simple.

Now is the time to look at what your identity really is, not what you'd like it to be.

I AM ____________________   I AM ____________________

I AM ____________________   I AM ____________________

I AM ____________________   I AM ____________________

I AM ____________________   I AM ____________________

I AM ____________________   I AM ____________________

Some of the statements you've just created will feel more positive than others, which is fine. Consider that from the identity's perspective, there's no good, bad, or best. It's as though you have programmed yourself with these I AM statements, and your identity is consistently carrying out that program to the letter, without judgment or analysis.

Of course, anything can be cleared, and identity work is no exception. Drop me a line if you'd like my help in shifting an identity statement.

Incidentally, the work you just completed—finishing the I AM statements above—is honest, introspective work most people never do. Now that you've brought these I AM statements to light, you will likely begin to notice how pervasive they are. They must be, right? They're part of who you are. These traits will show up in areas of your life you hadn't previously considered. This is part of the fun!

The trick will be to notice them without judgment, which would sound or feel like, "Wow, I really *am* loud!" versus "Ewww. I can't believe I'm so loud. Have I always been this obnoxious?"

For the next few days, see if you can become more aware of your I AM beliefs by paying attention to your words, thoughts, and actions. When you notice an I AM belief playing out, think to yourself, "How very interesting," which can help prevent you from slipping into self-judgment.

Activating the Solar Plexus

This exercise has many benefits, but the real purpose of it is to identify who you are and how you are, so that you can harness those assets to move forward.

As you take some time to complete the following statements, keep your I AM statements in mind, as these will help to guide your answers appropriately. Unless of course one of your

                69

statements is I AM inappropriate. Just kidding, heh heh. I know, I know. I said no judgment. Did I mention that one of my identity statements is I AM clever?

These statements combine the sense of self with self-love, which will lead us beautifully into the final exercise in this section. Enjoy!

I love that I am _________________________________.

I love that I can _________________________________.

I love that I have _________________________________.

I love that I know _________________________________.

Other people compliment me on my _________________________________.

People appreciate my _________________________________.

I am often acknowledged for _________________________________.

I appreciate that I am _________________________________.

I am grateful for my _________________________________.

I have always loved that I _________________________________.

I would like to learn to be more _________________________________,

      and _________________________________,

      and _________________________________.

I would like to learn to appreciate myself for _________________________________.

I deserve to be recognized for my _________________________________.

I am learning to love myself for _________________________________.

The area where I most desire growth is _________________________________.

Thank you, Source, for helping me _________________________________.

This year, I have the potential to _________________________________.

By this time next year, I will be _________________________.

Anything else you wish to add?

____

Level 7: Sacral Chakra

About the Sacral Chakra

The sacral chakra is located just below and behind your naval. This is the center associated with pleasure, sexuality, creativity, and abundance. Interestingly enough, those who are blocked sexually are often blocked creatively, and vice versa. Got no partner at the moment? Might just have to take care of business yourself, if you know what I mean. I'm not trying to be crass; you cannot feel balanced and totally at peace if one of your chakras is blocked, and this includes the sex chakra.

For those with a defined sacral center (as per Human Design), commitments are absolute. A defined sacral center means it will be very difficult—if not impossible—to break a commitment once you enter into it. Even if keeping the commitment makes you miserable and uncomfortable. Those with an undefined sacral center will have a greater sense of freedom around commitments, finding themselves able to weave in and out of agreements in a manner that baffles those with a defined sacrum.

The color most often associated with the sacral chakra is orange, which is the color of expansion.

Vision Board

A vision board or dream board can be as simple and inexpensive as a sheet of white poster board, or as elaborate as a video slideshow, but the goal is the same: to create a visual representation of your goals and intentions. This works because it impresses the images upon your subconscious mind, which facilitates faster manifestation.

Remember: it's far more effective to use a photo of the new car you want if *your* photo is included, as opposed to simply pasting an image of the car by itself. This helps your subconscious mind take possession of what you want.

I recommend using a balance of words and photos, as the combination tends to produce better results than one or the other alone. If you Google "vision board examples" and select "images" you can find some great ideas for the overall look of a vision board. Be sure to prominently feature your **Boom word** on your vision board!

For most, this is a very pleasant and fun experience. Others (especially those who are creatively blocked) may dread this activity. Perfectionists will procrastinate beginning this process, with the unbearable burden of worrying over how to make it perfectly perfect. If you want to beat procrastination right now, get started immediately on your vision board. Action beats procrastination every time. Don't overthink it, just get started. Every baby step counts.

NOTE: It is very likely that in this dream board process, you will think of new items to add to your Fireworks 100 List. Be sure to flip back and jot them down as you think of these, while fresh in your mind.

My BOOM word for the year is: _______________________________

What new things/toys/possessions do I most want to have by this time next year?

____

____

____

What new experiences do I most want to have (travel locations, shows, excursions, etc.)?

____

____

____

Which people do I most want to connect with? (celebrities, experts, new friends and associates, new relationships, helpers, etc.)

____

____

What else will be new in my life in a year? (new skills, hobbies, career, things to learn and master, achievements, accolades, etc.)

____

____

What would life look like if today were a perfect mirror of your vision board?

____

____

____

____

The following questions may help with your vision board, but the real reason they appear here is to support you in completing your Fireworks 100. Don't get too hung up on my suggestions; just have fun imagining the possibilities!

Sports I'd like to try (parasailing, snowboarding, racquetball, bocce ball, bowling, badminton, scuba diving, dodge ball, etc.):

____

____

National landmarks and points of interest I'd love to visit in my country:

____

____

International landmarks and points of interests I want to visit this year:

____

____

Plays and theater shows I'd love to see:

____

____

Comedians I'd like to watch in person:

____

____

Musicians and bands I'd love to see live in concert this year:

____

____

Events I want to attend this year:

____

____

People I'd love to spend time with this year:

____

____

Movies I've never seen but always wanted to:

____

____

New foods or cuisines I'd like to try:

____

____

____

Restaurants where I'd love to dine:

____

____

Specific dishes I'd be willing to cook for the first time this year:

____

____

Specific projects I've started that I'd love to complete this year:

____

____

Classes I want to take this year:

____

____

New things I'd like to learn this year (how to write a novel, fly a plane, tie boating knots, play an instrument, learn to bake, whittle, whistle, etc.):

____

____

Books I want to read this year:

____

____

Experiences I'd love to have this year, for the first time, or the first in a long time):

____

____

____

Money Goals

Okay, let's talk about money.

I want to receive $_________________________________ in the next 12 months.

My goal represents a _________________ % increase over my prior year's earnings.

To calculate that percentage: subtract your actual earnings from last year from your goal for this year, and then divide that number into your actual for last year, and then multiply by one hundred to convert to a percentage. In other words:

$$(\textbf{New Goal} - \textbf{Last Year Actual}) / \textbf{Last Year Actual} \times 100$$

For example, if you earned $80,000 last year and your goal is $120,000, then here's the calculation:

$$\$120,000 - \$80,000 = \$40,000$$
$$\$40,000 / \$80,000 = 0.5$$
$$0.5 \times 100 = 50\%$$

In this example, your new goal would represent a **50% increase** over last year.

It doesn't matter if you use pre-tax or take-home pay numbers, just keep it consistent for both years in your calculation.

What's the "y" in Money for?

Money for the sake of money is rarely enough motivation to carry a person through to achievement. There's a "y" at the end of "money" to remind you to focus on your "why," as opposed to just focusing on the money itself.

Without knowing what the extra money is for, it's unlikely that you'll achieve a higher income, and even if you do, you're likely to blow it in a way that doesn't create any kind of lasting influence on your life or the lives of others. Then, when it's time to pay taxes, you're left thinking, "I made *how much* last year? Where did all that money go?"

What's your **why** for money? Let's get clear about that right now.

I'm excited to create this additional money so that I can:

____

____

____

Achieving all of this makes me feel:

____

____

____

Next, it's important to look at the potential obstacles that could be in your way, so that you can create a strategy for handling blocks. Before you address the next question, read through all of your money answers above and notice what comes up in your mind.

What blocks, doubts, fears, or limiting beliefs arise when I think about achieving my new money goals?

____

____

____

Now you can either clear those blocks or create strategic ways to combat them. For example, let's say that one of your fears is that you won't have enough time to complete the necessary action to get the extra money. You could either clear that fear, or you could create a time management strategy to help ensure you have enough time. You could carve out time in your schedule, and pre-schedule the milestones and actions required to complete the necessary work.

Take some time to address these blocks now.

★ ★ ★

Can you begin to imagine all the ways that you could achieve this new money goal? Here are a few examples to get you thinking (let's say your new goal is to add $20,000 to your income this year):

> Sign twenty additional clients at $1,000 net earnings each.

> Sign ten additional clients at $2,000 each.

> Create an "ultimate package" for which you sign two clients at $10,000 each.

> Land ten speaking gigs at $2,000 each.

> Create a workshop and sell 40 spots at $500 each.

> Attract one part-time consulting client who pays $20,000 for the year.

> Take on a part-time sales job.

> Ask for a $20,000 raise.

> Start a business on the side where you generate $1667 profit per month.

> Ask current clients for referrals and offer a referral incentive.

If you do not currently own a business or you have a salaried or hourly-pay job, you will either have to get more creative about what you could sell or do on the side, or you would need to revisit your goal and shoot for a smaller increase over last year. Your brain must believe it's possible, and that it *can* happen, even if you don't have all the exact details as to *how* it will happen. This is the first step to ensuring it *will* happen.

The point of the next brainstorming exercise is to get your mind thinking of all the ways the increase in your income *is possible*. This is actually one of my specialties, and one of my favorite things to do for my clients.

It's so easy to fall into a rut, and sometimes it takes an outside perspective to say, "Hey, you're doing great! Would you like to be doing even better with just one or two small changes?" My entrepreneurial, executive, and sales rep clients are blown away when I give them an idea they've never thought of, even though the idea may seem obvious once I point it out to them. It's just a matter of perspective. I am an MBA with more than twenty years of experience as an entrepreneur. Plus I'm an excellent strategist and I'm highly intuitive, so when you combine all of that with a fresh objective perspective, it's a recipe for amazingly simple yet effective ideas that can be executed immediately.

Your brain is a powerful asset, and it works for you 24/7. I like to give my brain problems to solve in the background, as I go about my daily activities. The subconscious mind loves to solve problems and it's remarkably good at it—far better than the conscious mind, in fact. Brainstorming a list of ways you can earn a specific amount of additional income triggers a few benefits:

> Puts your subconscious mind to work figuring out how to make it happen.

> Demonstrates to you that it's possible, *and* there are several ways it can happen.

> Helps to diminish or remove doubts that you have about your ability to achieve it.

> Can show you if your goals are too pie-in-the-sky, or if they are actually doable.

> Puts you in a mental position of "this is really happening" as opposed to setting a money goal with no substance to support its actualization.

> Assists you in creating an action plan to achieve the goal.

Brainstorming Time

There are many ways you can achieve your income goal for this year. Brainstorm at least twenty ideas:

1. ____

2. ____

3. ____

4. ____

5. ____

6. ____

7. ____

8. ____

9. ____

10. ____

11. ____

12. ____

13. ____

14. ____

15. ____

16. ____

17. ____

18. ____

19. ____

20. ____

If you own a business, what specific business goals do you have for the next twelve months? For example, you may wish to grow your social media following by a certain percentage, increase your client base, launch a new product or service, author or co-author a book, join a professional organization, etc. If so, it's a good idea to note where you are now with these, so you can check your progress as the year continues. For example, if you want to grow your private Facebook group membership to 1000, it would be helpful to record here what your current membership is, so that you can see what kind of increase you're aiming for.

What would you like to benchmark as of today?

____

____

____

____

____

____

Aligning Your Work with Your Core Values

Entire books have been written on the subject of **core values.** In the broadest of strokes, your core values are the principles and ideas that underpin how you move through life. It is what you are most attracted to, and the guidelines against which you measure satisfaction and value.

The value of core values

If you know your core values, you can use them to guide you in creating your business strategy for the year.

For example, one of my core values is **fun.** Writing books is not a huge moneymaker for me, but it's fun. And there are secondary benefits, because it helps people find me online and get introduced to my work, which leads to them purchasing my courses and becoming private clients.

I hosted my own telesummit once, and it was not fun. Parts of it were fun, but mostly it wasn't. It did okay financially, but even if it had been wildly successful, I would not have wanted to do another because it just wasn't fun, and fun is one of the attributes I value most.

When fun is present (along with my other core values such as: **excellence, results, learning, and purpose)** I am at my best. If the telesummit had been substantially lucrative, then I likely would have looked for a way to make it fun. But it didn't, so I chalked it up to a learning experience and adjusted my strategy for the following year. Capisce?

Looking for guidance?

If you don't know your core values, you can use your BOOM word to guide you. Or check out my Core Values videos on YouTube. **YouTube.com/amyscottgrant**

If your Boom word is "expansion" then look for ways that you can expand your reach and your business. If your Boom word is "peace" then take a look at the products and services that *didn't* make an impact on your bottom line. If you have stress around any of these, can you outsource them or simply stop offering them altogether?

If you'd like my help in leveraging your business to get more of what you want, give me a call or see the offer at the end of this book. See what I did there? That's how you leverage the sale of a book into something more impactful. Next we'll move on to our final chakra: the root.

Level 8: Root

About the Root Chakra

The root chakra is located at the base of your spine at the tailbone (coccyx). C'mon, say it out loud with me, it's fun. "Coccyx." If you say it three times fast, it starts to sound dirty. Just kidding. This chakra is dead serious: it's your foundation of support and stability. A well-balanced root chakra means you are grounded, centered, and secure.

The root chakra is all about getting your basic survival needs met: food, shelter, clothing, and enough money to cover your bills. When this chakra is unbalanced, illness can occur, or worse. Balancing this chakra brings safety and a sense of security. The color most often associated with the root chakra is a dark or ruddy red.

At the risk of sounding like a total dork, I will confess to you now that I love, love, love my root chakra. Before I dove into my intuitive gifts, my root was extremely blocked. Today it grounds me 24/7, effortlessly. It works so hard for me and for everyone I heal, and it is a huge reason that I am able to cause miracles.

The energy in the room shifts when I walk into it, and as much as I'd like to believe it's charm or charisma, it's really as simple as this: I hold a massive grounding energy all around me, and when people meet me, they feel it. Thank you, root chakra. You rock.

Grounding Exercise

Remember that "Connecting to Source" exercise we did way back in the Crown chakra section? If you did it, you grounded yourself. Simple, right? Here's a recap of the grounding part, so you can try your hand at it again.

> *Stand with your feet planted firmly on the ground, weight distributed evenly between both feet. Relax your knees. Close your eyes and relax. Relax your jaw, your shoulders, and your tongue. Imagine there is a cord, any kind of cord or rope or string you like, running from the base of your spine all the way down to the center of the earth. This cord connects you, and you feel safe and grounded because of it.*

That's it. Now you're grounded. Of course, getting grounded isn't like getting a tattoo. You don't get grounded and stay that way forever. It's more like brushing your teeth. Unless you do it regularly, stuff gets icky.

How can you tell if you're <u>not</u> grounded? Here are a few indicators:

- Feeling overwhelmed

- Feeling like you can't settle down or sit still

- Feeling like you can't focus or concentrate

- Feeling like a lot of stuff is coming at you and you're not sure what to address first

- Feeling upset or experiencing any strong unpleasant emotion

- Feeling stressed out, maxed out, spaced out, or tapped out

- Feeling like you're not centered, or your head is in the clouds

- Feeling unsafe or even threatened

- Getting a headache after being around other people or crowds

- Feeling like you need a minute to think, some quiet, or some time to yourself, *pronto*

Get the picture? Good. Here are a few other ways you can ground yourself:

- **Go outside and connect with nature.** This could be as simple as a leisurely walk, watching a sunset, or gazing at the clouds. Or it could be more interactive, like gardening, photographing trees, hunting for cool rocks, or walking barefoot in the grass. Just stepping outdoors provides a swift grounding effect for many people.

- **Use this book.** Because (spoiler alert) I energetically built grounding into this book. I'm cool like that. You might have noticed this book relaxes you, or makes you feel safe and cozy. If you're naturally grounded, you might *not* have noticed because you were already grounded. Either way, you're welcome.

- **Embrace earthy colors like chocolate brown and brick red**. Wear them, choose stones and jewelry in these colors, and get a warm, cozy blanket in a grounding color for your bed or your favorite chair.

- **Speaking of chocolate, eat some.** Yes, I am telling you chocolate is good for grounding. When I write, I always have some good quality dark chocolate handy because when I'm writing, I'm more or less channeling, so the chocolate ensures that I stay grounded during the process. Um, yeah. That's totally why I eat chocolate.

I'm inviting you to get grounded—not only during this Root chakra section, but all throughout your life. If you want to become masterful at grounding, pop over to Amazon and get yourself a copy of my book, *The Lightworker's Guide to Grounding Energy.*

After that, why not take a couple of minutes to pop some grounding reminders into your calendar?

How often, you ask? Good question. How often would you say you experience the indicators we covered above? Daily? Couple times a week? Maybe once or twice a month? Well, then there's your answer as to how often you should remind yourself to ground. If you have a digital calendar, schedule a recurring event as a reminder and you'll be good to go.

Meeting Your Needs

The root chakra is all about getting your needs met, so let's take a look at what you will need in order to create your most successful year possible. We'll start with something easy: **your home.**

What do you love about where you live? It might be the location, the size or spaciousness, the decor, the furnishings, the photographs, the textures, the colors, the scents, the warmth, the views, the yard, the neighbors, the hot tub, the quietness, or anything at all.

____

____

____

Now think about how you'd like your space to feel. If your home could feel any way you wanted, how would you want it to feel?

____

____

____

On a scale of 1-10 (1 = no way José, 10 = duh, ob-vi), how closely does the current feeling of your home match the desired vibe? _______

If you answered 8 or less, what specific changes could you make to create more of the desired feeling in your home? Please list at least three.

1.

2.

3.

Excellent. Now let's move on to your time. What would you love to spend less time (or no time) doing?

____

____

____

What would you love to spend more time doing?

____

____

____

On a scale of 1-10 (1 = completely dissatisfied, 10 = totally satisfied), how satisfied are you with the way your time is currently spent? _______

If you answered 8 or less, what specific changes could you make to spend less time doing things that bring you little to no satisfaction and more time doing things that bring you great satisfaction? Please list at least three.

1.

2.

3.

How many hours a week on average do you spend working or thinking about work? Be sure to include time spent on email. ______ hours per week

On a scale of 1-10 (1 = completely dissatisfied, 10 = totally satisfied), how satisfied are you with your answer to the previous question? _______

If you answered 8 or less, list at least three changes you could implement immediately that would allow you to spend less time working and more time enjoying life. (HINT: What could you realistically outsource right now? What could you eliminate entirely?)

1.

2.

3.

Next, we'll address money. In a word or two, how would you describe your current relationship with money?

____

If your relationship with money could feel any way you wanted it to, how would you want it to feel?

____

____

On a scale of 1-10 (1 = completely dissatisfied, 10 = totally satisfied), how satisfied are you with your overall relationship with money? _______

If you answered 8 or less, what specific changes could you make to begin to move toward the relationship you want with money, while moving away from what you don't like about the current status? Please list at least three.

1.

2.

3.

Speaking of relationships… what is your primary relationship at this time? This could be a significant other or spouse, a business partner, a best friend, a sibling or parent, etc.

____

In a word or two, how would you describe this relationship?

____

Is it working or not working? Do you want to make it work or move on?

____

____

If you want to stay and make it work, what would have to change in order for it to work? (And don't say the other person, because you and I both know that ain't gonna happen.)

____

____

____

If you want to move on, what would it take for you to walk away?

____

____

Do you want this relationship to be your primary relationship? In other words, are you happy with the fact that this is the person you spend the most amount of time with? Circle YES or NO.

YES   NO

If you answered no, what can you do to change that?

____

____

____

By the way, if the word you used to describe your current primary relationship was "toxic," please don't try to make it work. Just cut your losses and move on. You're not serving yourself or the other person by dragging out the inevitable.

In a word or two, how would you describe how you feel about your body right now? (This can be from any perspective you chose: physical appearance, weight, health, well-being, fitness, allergies, etc.)

____

If you could create any kind of feeling at all about your body, how would you love to feel?

____

____

____

On a scale of 1-10 (1 = completely dissatisfied, 10 = totally satisfied), how satisfied are you currently with your body? ________

If you answered less than 8, what specific changes could you make to move toward the body you want? (HINT: it *might* be more about self-love and acceptance, and less about physical transformation.) Please list no more than three.

1.

2.

3.

What else do you require in order to be supported in achieving your goals in the next twelve months? Please list it here.

____

____

____

Do you spend your time in congruence with your priorities? Let's find out.

What is the single most important thing in your life?

____

____

____

____

Use the following chart to detail an average day, approximately. Be honest!

Hours you actually sleep, on average (include naps) _______________

Amount of time you spend preparing and eating breakfast _______________

Amount of time you spend on your personal hygiene (brushing teeth, showering, bathroom, makeup, hair, exercising, etc.) _______________

Amount of time you spend driving (yourself, kids, etc.) _______________

Amount of time you spend on email and social media _______________

Amount of time you spend studying or in school or classes _______________

Amount of time you spend working _______________

Amount of time you spend preparing and eating lunch _______________

Amount of time you spend preparing and eating snacks/coffee/etc. _______________

Amount of time you spend preparing and eating dinner _______________

Amount of time you spend taking care of your home (laundry, cleaning, tidying up, performing yard work or maintenance, dishes, reading mail, paying bills, handling paperwork, etc.) _______________

Amount of time you spend watching TV in an average day _______________

Amount of time you'd call "waste" (video games, Pinterest, etc.) _______________

Amount of time you spend in pure enjoyment in other activities (spending time
with friends, reading for pleasure, having a soak, going out,
engaging in hobbies or arts that you love, etc.)   ___________

Amount of time you spend in self-care: meditation, massage, etc.   ___________

Now add up your total to see how close you are to 24 hours: ___________

How much time is missing? (Subtract your total from 24)   ___________

What else do you spend time doing? Fill in the activities that make up the gap:

____

____

____

We could categorize where most of our time goes like this:

Personal Essentials - time during your day spent to meet essential needs like bathing, dressing, personal hygiene, eating, sleeping, etc.

Personal Benefits - time spent taking care of yourself beyond mere survival needs: exercising, inspirational reading, meditation, prayer, massage, quality time with loved ones, etc.

Productive Work - any action that moves you toward the accomplishment of a specific goal.

Non-productive Work - commute time, B.S. meetings, brown-nosing, coffee breaks, non-business lunches, "shooting the breeze" with co-workers, drive time, etc.

Relaxation - leisurely walks, golf, swimming for fun (as opposed to swimming for exercise, which would be counted under "personal benefits,") catnaps, games, reading for pleasure, fun times with loved ones, hobbies, etc.

Donations - volunteer work, helping others in need, PTA, church work, and any other activity where you volunteer your time.

Escapes - any action (or inaction) you use to "wind down," by escaping the pressures and busy-ness of the day. Includes time spent reading the newspaper, watching television, gossiping, aimlessly surfing the internet, playing video games, complaining, and any other activity used to procrastinate or "kill time."

Now you can look at your chart to see which category occupies most of your time.

Are you surprised by your results? Some people feel a bit disappointed by a high number of non-productive work hours and/or the low number of personal benefits hours. Now that you can see where your time is going, it's easier to see what kinds of small changes can be implemented to create big shifts and to get more satisfaction from your life.

What specifically did you learn about how you currently spend your time?

____

____

____

Does your breakdown of how you spend your time align with what you identified (at the beginning of this section) as the number one priority in your life? If not, how does that feel?

____

____

Where specifically do you see potential for improvement?

____

____

What activities could you remove completely or simply stop doing?

____

____

____

____

Is it difficult for you to ask for help? If so, why do you think that is? What's stopping or blocking you from asking for the help you need?

____

____

____

Which activities could be outsourced or delegated?

____

____

Whom could you ask for help?

____

____

____

Is there anything you're doing in person that could be done with greater ease and/or less time if you did it online instead?

____

____

____

What could you realistically stop doing in person and start doing online?

____

____

____

Next, let's talk about consolidating tasks.

Could you designate a two-hour block each week for household stuff, instead of catching it hit-or-miss throughout the week? You might consider batch cooking, designating one laundry day per week, planning errands to avoid doubling back, catching up on business calls during a long drive or while waiting in the carline to pick up the kids, or hiring a sitter for a couple of hours in order to handle some business tasks. I consolidate business activities like "batch recording" videos. If I've already done the hair and makeup, I might as well leverage it by shooting multiple videos with a couple of wardrobe changes for variety. To further leverage it even more, I'll typically schedule lunch with a friend on the same day because hey, I already look good, so why not?

Finally, would you like to know one of the simplest ways to create more time in your life? It's simple, but not always easy. But it's most definitely worth a try.

Think before you commit.

For some of us, the "yes, of course" is already out of our mouths before our brain has had a chance to process the question. Many times, we haven't even considered whether or not we *want* to say yes, or what the specific expectations are, or the potential ramifications for saying "no." This leads to over committing and ultimately, overwhelm.

When you feel overwhelmed, you become ungrounded and then you cannot perform at your best. Which means, if you have any underlying beliefs about not being good enough (and most people do), you can bet these will surface as a result of over committing. Perhaps it is your need to prove that you are in fact good enough that has you saying "yes" so quickly in the first place. Whatever the reason, over committing sucks and leads to major stress and ultimately, feeling as deflated as if you'd let someone down.

Simple solution: think before you commit.

In all the years since I've started the "pre-commitment consideration" as I like to call it, I've never once had anyone become angry or upset when they asked me to do something and I responded with, "Let me think about it and get back with you."

The absolute worst that's ever come of it (and it isn't even bad) is that they may say, "I need an answer from you by tomorrow," which means I only have a day to decide. That's it—that's the worst that could happen! And in most cases, the response is something more like "take your time" or "Do you think you could let me know within a week or two?" Then, when I come back two days later with my mindfully chosen answer, I wind up looking like a goddess, even if say no. Which I don't mind one bit.

We "yes" people like to think we must answer immediately. Problem? Yes, yes, I've got a solution! Even if I don't, I'll stay up all night to think of a totally badass awesome one! We stress ourselves out for nothing.

The next time you are asked to do something, whether it's going to lunch or spearheading the new Robinson project, practice saying, "let me think about it and get back to you," or "can I get back with you on that?" and watch what happens.

Action Time!

With your highlighter in hand, take a few minutes to review your lists of possible changes from the two prior exercises in this section. Highlight the ones **you are ready and willing to implement in the next twelve months.** Then grab your day planner or smartphone and schedule in those actions. If one of your best ideas is to "spend two hours of 'me' time each week," (a superb idea, by the way…highly recommended), put a "schedule 2 hours of ME time" reminder on your calendar now for every Sunday night (or whenever you're most likely to follow through on it) from now until a year from now. Then whenever you see that on your schedule, do it.

I don't know about you, but when I see the same thing on my calendar week after week, sometimes if it's not essential, I conveniently overlook it. But when there's a personal note from me to me ("remember when you said you wanted to practice more self-care?") it's a lot harder to ignore, which means it's much more likely to get done. So add in these love notes if you need 'em.

Replace your wasted TV time with productive time—this is how to create what you want. If you said you need to relax more, then schedule something more relaxing than television (for example, just about anything). How about yoga, meditation, naps, hot tubs or Epson soaks, a foot massage or pedicure, reading a novel, or listening to soothing music? What you choose depends on what is most relaxing to you. The point here is to calendar it in, because you will significantly increase your chances of success when you simply write it down. Scheduling time to make it happen enhances your success rate even more.

Changes to Calendar:

____

____

____

____

Now off you go, you powerhouse of organization and commitment. Happy change scheduling!

All done? Excellent! Here's your immediate reward for completing the above: you get to move on to one of the most fun exercises in this entire book. Together we'll forecast your year. Fun, fun, fun! But first, be sure you've got all those changes calendared.

Level 9: Moving Forward

Time for Some Fun

Here's how to play "forecasting with cards." Draw twelve cards from your favorite tarot deck in order to get an energetic feel for each month of your coming year.

I know what you may be thinking. If you've seen any of my free pendulum training videos at **http://YouTube.com/amyscottgrant** or read *Pendulum Mojo*, then you've heard me say repeatedly that prediction-type questions are not valid.

It's true, and I stand by that statement.

However, card pulls are different. You can use any kind of spiritual oracle deck to inquire about the energy of a particular situation. "Show me the energy around my love life" is different from asking a specific predictive question like "will I get married this year?"

While it's true that things are always in flux, I have found that when we ask about the energy around a situation, it tends to remain fairly static unless we intentionally change something.

For example, if you ask about the energy around your love life, and the cards come back with a bleak reading, you might then be inspired to make some changes. Perhaps you change your look with a new hairstyle or a wardrobe makeover. Maybe you take a course or read a book about becoming more desirable on the dating scene, or you choose to put yourself out there a bit more.

Then, after you've made those changes, you could shuffle up and do another card pull and ask again about the energy around your love life, and if your efforts have effected a change, you would likely receive a completely different card reading.

This is precisely why I've waited until the end of this workbook to recommend forecasting with cards. We've already evaluated and looked at what changes you can make, and you've already committed to (and scheduled) many of those changes. (Um, you did do all that, right?) Now is the perfect time to check in on the energy around your coming year.

Forecasting with Cards

There are countless oracle decks to choose from and you are sure to find a set that speaks to you. You can find fairy cards, dragon cards, new age cards, energy cards, angel cards, crystal cards, and tons of others. Yes, there's the Spiritual Ass Kicker Discovery Deck, but that's not for forecasting, it's for "retrocasting." I created that deck to find the root cause of any block.

My personal favorite deck for the past several years is *The Psychic Tarot* by John Holland. I received this as a gift on my birthday in 2013, and I've used this deck exclusively for forecasting ever since. I've given several as gifts because everybody loves this deck. I can recommend it without reservation (despite the fact that I won't earn a cent if you buy one) and it comes with an excellent pocket-sized guidebook that explains each card thoroughly and succinctly.

If you are new to cards, I recommend practicing for a while (instructions are typically provided with each deck) and remember to shuffle thoroughly before you pull your forecast for the year. Just like a new deck of playing cards, a brand-new spiritual deck should be broken in a bit before you do your forecasting for the year.

Would you prefer to have your forecasting done for you by an objective third-party intuitive? Perhaps by yours truly? Ask and it is given. You can visit this link **http://AskAmyAnything.com/forecast** to learn how to get a custom video of your personal forecast/reading (also includes a birds-eye view of your card spread).

Unless you don't work and have no intention of working, I strongly recommend that you **pull two complete and independent spreads.** This means pulling a twelve-card personal spread, taking a photo of it, then returning those cards to the deck, shuffling thoroughly, and then pulling a completely separate twelve-card spread for your career or business.

I like to ask my question or hold an intention while I'm shuffling, and then place the cards one by one in order, and then take a photo of all twelve cards. This is an example of what I might be thinking as I'm shuffling:

"Please show me the energy around the next twelve months." Then I would think "April" (or whatever the upcoming month may be) as I pull the first card, "May" as I pull the second card, etc., until I've pulled twelve cards.

Once all the cards are pulled, I snap a photo with my iPhone, record them on the worksheet, jot down a few thoughts, plus any intuitive hits I get while reading the card. Be sure to write the name of the month somewhere inside each box!

You can fan the cards out face down and pick one at a time at random, or you can shuffle and pick twelve sequentially. It really just depends on what feels optimal to you at the time. In my opinion, you cannot over-shuffle oracle cards.

If you're highly analytical, it's often best to have someone else do the card pull for you. If you already have some experience with oracle cards, this will be a breeze for you. Remember to ground before you begin. Now turn the page and happy forecasting!

Did you enjoy forecasting? Or perhaps you are now awaiting the results of your done-for-you card reading from me. If you're currently waiting, you can finish out the rest of the workbook while you wait, and then return to this page once you have received your forecast(s).

Remember, the cards merely suggest the energy surrounding each month in your coming year. They are not immutable. If you are concerned about a certain month, you can always do some clearing work or see what is available to shift the energy surrounding that month. But remember, ups and downs are a part of life, so it's unlikely that you'll have an entire year of nothing but ups. Forecasting is a great tool because it helps you to prepare for (notice I did *not* say "obsess over") potential downs and feel ready when they arrive.

I like to revisit the pages of my forecast every month, to see how the prior month's forecast measured up to what I actually experienced, and to see what is likely to arise in the current month and the following month. It helps me in planning my business launches, my personal travel, and other key decisions. Of course, I always recommend checking in with your preferred Truth Testing method when making any significant decision. But you're already doing that, right? (Seriously, have you read *Pendulum Mojo* yet?)

Which months' forecasts feel the most exciting to you? What specifically are you looking forward to?

____

____

____

As you look through your forecast for the next twelve months, does anything concern you? If so, what are some specific actions you could take to resolve those concerns?

____

____

____

____

With your plans for the year in mind, look through your personal and business forecast for clues as to which months would be optimal for which goals, and then use your preferred Truth Testing method to check in and verify.

For example, if July appears to be an excellent month for travel or an extended time away from work, and one of things on your goal list for the year is a trip to Barcelona, then you can check in and ask, "All things considered, is it optimal to go to Barcelona in July?" If you get a no, don't panic—it could mean any number of things. Perhaps there's someplace more optimal than Barcelona for you, or you'll take two big trips this year (one to Barcelona, and somewhere else in July), or perhaps something is likely to change, making a different month more optimal for Barcelona. But can you see how it helps to know the expected energy around each month, so that you can plan your goals accordingly?

Excellent. Now look back through your goals and make some notes on your forecasting spread as to which months might be most optimal for which goals. I like to do this by simply putting one or two words that represent the goal under the month. For example, if I am planning to buy a new car, and the August forecast says "out with the old and in with the new," I might write "new car?" under August as a reminder to myself. Take a few minutes to do this now.

Are there any messages from your spread that are confusing or mysterious to you? If so, take a few minutes to write down your questions here, so your subconscious mind can get to work. Expect that the answers will come to you at the optimal time.

____

____

____

Do you have any additional concerns? For example, an impending divorce or historically "slow season" in your business. If so, you can pull additional cards to address these issues, or write your questions and concerns below so that you can clear or address these after your mind has taken a day or two to process.

____

____

____

Anything else on your mind after reviewing your forecasts? Capture your thoughts and feelings here for later reference.

____

____

____

____

____

____

Hot Tips for Cool Results

Wow, congratulations! You are nearly finished and I'm so very proud of you and the work you've done to energetically and mindfully map out your year. Especially considering how pivotal this next year is shaping up to be. Boom!

How do you feel? If by chance you feel overwhelmed, take a moment to ground yourself and then schedule in some more action. Once it's in your calendar, it can leave your mind and give you some mental peace. It's the easiest way to shift out of overwhelm and into action. Additionally, take a step today—no matter how small. Action brings feelings of empowerment and accomplishment, and quickly dissolves any stress or feelings of being inundated.

Once you're feeling good, check out the following tips for success.

☑ Tip #1

Flip back through this workbook and complete any exercises or pages you skipped. Must you do this step? No. If you do this step, will it dramatically increase your chances of success? Yes. Especially if you are resisting for some reason. _What? Me, resist?_ I swear, I can almost hear you.

☑ Tip #2

Schedule periodic "progress check-ins" on your calendar or day planner. Personally, I like to check in every month, but it's really a personal preference. The purpose of these check-ins is to see how you're doing overall. Last year, when I did my first check-in, I took a pink Sharpie and drew a fat checkmark next to everything I had accomplished so far on my Fireworks 100 list. It always amazes me how many items on that list get done, simply by identifying them and writing them down. The manifesting power of our minds is simply astonishing, isn't it?

By the time you complete your first check-in, you are likely to see dramatic changes in how you spend your time (providing you implemented the changes you came up with). The awareness that you're investing your time more wisely will bring you greater satisfaction as you move through your day and your year.

Finally, the check-ins help you renew your commitment to the unfinished (or as of yet untouched) items on your list. I find that my last few check-ins of the year help me to focus, prioritize what's remaining, and buckle down before the year runs out. I am always astonished when results come together at the eleventh hour, simply because I refused to give up.

☑ Tip #3

Want to see how your forecast actually pans out? Then take a minute to schedule monthly check-in reminders on your calendar to review your forecast for the upcoming month, and compare the prior month's forecast to what actually took place.

☑ Tip #4

Things change because you change. This is, in essence, the entire basis of my Ripple Magic program. Like casting a pebble into a pond, one change within you causes an outwardly rippling effect that impacts everyone you come into contact with. The more you transform yourself, the more ripples of change you create. As you improve, the people in your life improve (or they don't stick around). It's magical, really. Boom is a powerfully effective tool for transformation, but it is just one tool. If you want more, check out the "What's Next" section at the back of this book. If you want it all, take a look at the "Before You Go…" section. But even if the only thing you do is to complete this personal almanac, you have already cast the pebble and created an impact. Congratulations!

☑ Tip #5

Have you ever written a letter from your future self? You can write or type this letter, but I prefer to handwrite mine because there's just something anciently delicious about receiving a handwritten message, and it's even better when it comes from the one who knows me best!

Start with a clean page and imagine you have achieved everything you set out to accomplish the next twelve months. From this future perspective of achievement, write a letter *from* that future version of you *to* today's version of you. You can write anything you want, anything at all. You may wish to refer back to your answers from the Future Self exercise in Section 3.

After you write a letter from your future self, you want to make sure that you read it approximately one year from now. You could put it in a safe place, and (unless you are the lucky kind of person who can remember where you stashed something twelve months ago) put a tickler reminder on your calendar, including the location of the letter so you can find it. Or, you could seal it in an envelope and staple it to the inside cover of this book. That way, you'll notice it whenever you do your progress check-ins. Have fun with this one!

☑ Tip #6

Because you change, your goals may change as well. The majority of what you've captured and clarified in this personal almanac will ring true for the year, but it's fine if some of it doesn't. One year from now, you will still be vastly more successful than you would have been without this focus and planning. This is why every consistently successful business in the world conducts regular, ongoing strategic planning. We do this because it works, period.

☑ Tip #7

Know that it won't all go exactly as planned. Sometimes it will turn out even better. Other times, it will go nowhere, and problems will occur that you could not have foreseen, even with the most accurate of forecasts. Focus on the good and keep moving forward, and you will achieve what you desire. Persistence is key.

☑ Tip #8

Always remember: **you frickin' rock.** You are comprised of Source Energy, which makes you all-powerful, all-connected, and all-awesome. If ever you doubt yourself or your goals (and you will, it happens to the best of us), tap into that inner infinite and refill your cup. Ground, connect to Source, and get what you need to keep moving forward. If you need help, ask for it.

☑ Tip #9

Want some support and camaraderie along the journey? Come and join my Club Clarity group on Facebook! It's a powerhouse of awesomeness, a private community of amazing individuals and support. Request to join the group here:

http://facebook.com/groups/askamyanything

☑ **Tip #10**

Remember to celebrate your wins! Whether it's hitting a specific milestone in a major goal, or accomplishing items on your Fireworks 100 list, every success is worth celebrating. You may even want to build in little rewards for achievements along the way. But when you accomplish something, don't just plow through it and grind on to the next thing—take a moment to pat yourself on the back for what you've done. We celebrate wins every Friday inside Club Clarity.

Just keep taking action.

Once you've calendared your reminders and end results, the next step is to take the bigger goals and projects and schedule in the accomplishment of your milestones along the way. Work backwards from the end. If you want to buy a car in August, you'll probably need to have the down payment saved up by the end of July, so you might want to schedule monthly or weekly reminders for saving for that, and June may be a good time to start shopping around and checking consumer reviews and visiting dealerships to test drive potential makes and models. All of these milestones can be calendared. Get the picture?

Remember, you've now completed all the hard work by finishing this personal almanac. The only thing left is to take action. Action does it!

What's on your mind right now?

____

____

____

____

____

____

____

____

Level 10: Launch Your Boom

Thank You

YOU DID IT! Thank for you taking the time to go through this entire *Boom* workbook. I hope you enjoyed this process as much as I've enjoyed putting it together for you, and I hope you didn't just skim the book, but that you took the time to actually work your way through the exercises. If you did, you are now locked and loaded for an extraordinary year! All that's left now to launch your BOOM is to start taking action.

By the way, if you enjoyed this book, please take a minute to write an honest review on Amazon or recommend this book via social media. Share your experiences with this personal almanac and invite others to check it out. This will assist people just like you who want a clear and fun way to mindfully create their year.

If you're willing, I'd love to have you come by my Facebook page at and share your Boom word with us. You never know how many people you may inspire and uplift simply by sharing this one simple word at:

http://facebook.com/groups/askamyanything

Want more Spiritual Ass Kicker stuff? Yes, please! Sign up for my weekly newsletter at

http://AmyScottGrant.com

Now that you've completed this workbook, you might be wondering what's next for you.

If you've planned a kickass year, and you **want some kickass help getting your blocks cleared,** why not schedule a private Get Your Mojo Back session with the Spiritual Ass Kicker?

http://SpiritualAssKicker.com/mojo

Want some help with your forecasting? Let me create a personal Video Card Reading for your next twelve months, either for your business, your personal life, or both. You get "forever access" to the videos, so you can refer back to them for guidance all year long.

http://AskAmyAnything.com/forecast

Would you like to have (or gift) a beautiful custom pendulum? These handmade creations are one of a kind, infused with vast quantities of love and healing energy, and we work with your guides and energy team to select colors and gemstones especially for you. Plus, when you make a purchase, you are supporting a teenage entrepreneur who is a big fan of *Shark Tank*. These pendulums make truly unique and memorable gifts for yourself or a loved one. Go ahead, "treat yo'self!"

http://CustomPendulums.com

Find more amazingly cool spiritual stuff to help you on your journey at:

http://Shop.AskAmyAnything.com

Would you like me to personally help you get unstuck, identify the root of your biggest blocks, and create a clear and specific plan to <u>permanently</u> dissolve those blocks for free?

In a private phone call with me, I will identify your underlying blocks (doubts, fears, limiting beliefs) and give you a list of these blocks so you can get clarity around what's <u>really</u> keeping you stuck. We'll also create a clear and specific plan to permanently dissolve each of these blocks so you can clear your crap, move forward quickly and powerfully, and avoid the pitfalls experienced by trying to clear blocks without a plan. I will also show you at least one very specific change you can make immediately so you can get instant relief.

I am a professional Spiritual Ass Kicker and I'm wildly enthusiastic about helping individuals like you to **get clear and get results.**

Some people, after talking to me, ask to join my year-long Ripple Magic program.

However, please understand **this is <u>not</u> a sales pitch in disguise.** If you ask to become a client, we can talk about it. If you ask me about Ripple Magic, we can talk about it. However, you will receive no sales pressure from me whatsoever. I promise you will find our conversation to be incredibly valuable.

I can't help everyone. I can only work with people who meet the following requirements.

First, **you must <u>not</u> be brand new to spiritual/energy/healing work.** If you just watched "The Secret" and your mind was blown, this is not for you.

Second, **you must be <u>on the verge</u> of what's next in your life.** If you're *not* feeling a strong pull to get clarity so that you can move forward in your career, relationships, and/or spiritual development, then this isn't for you.

Third, you must be **ready to create a substantial shift** for yourself and your life. If you're merely curious, then this is not for you.

If this sounds like you, then here's what to do next. Go to my website here **http://ripplemagic.com** to begin your application.

If all the available spots are filled by the time you apply, you can join the waitlist to be notified as space becomes available. If this sounds good, go to **RippleMagic.com** to get started and we'll set up a time to get connected.

Beyond the Fireworks 100 – Need space for more? Here you go, knock yourself out!

101.
102.
103.
104.
105.
106.
107.
108.
109.
110.
111.
112.
113.
114.
115.
116.
117.
118.
119.
120.
121.
122.
123.
124.
125.
126.
127.
128.
129.
130.
131.
132.
133.
134.
135.
136.
137.
138.
139.
140.
141.
142.

Thanks to her highly developed intuition and insatiable quest for human advancement, Spiritual Ass Kicker **Amy Scott Grant** has healed and helped hundreds of thousands of individuals in more than thirty countries through her speaking, writing, and mentoring. Her extraordinary gifts are peppered with a unique sense of humor and a healthy dose of levity.

In September 2013, Amy was inducted into the National Academy of Bestselling Authors and received the prestigious Quilly award at the Golden Gala Awards in Hollywood, California. She was selected as a Thought Leader of the Year Finalist in 2013.

Amy has created a number of successful books, courses, and digital products, including **Ripple Magic Transformation,** HIY: Heal It Yourself, and MindTime™ meditations for kids at KidCentered.com. You can find Amy's writing all over the internet, as well as in the bestselling book *Inspired Marketing* by Dr. Joe Vitale and Craig Perrine; the acclaimed *Chicken Soup for the Soul: Life Lessons for Mastering the Law of Attraction;* the #2 bestseller *Change Agents* with Brian Tracy; the youth spiritual novel *Annabel the Lost;* the *Spiritual Ass Kicker Discovery Deck; The Lightworker's Guide* series and more, available on Amazon.

Connect with Amy and discover what else is on the horizon at:

www.AskAmyAnything.com

1-2-3 Clarity! Banish Your Blocks, Doubts, Fears, and Limiting Beliefs Like a Spiritual Badass

Pendulum Mojo: How to Use Truth Testing for Clarity, Confidence, and Peace of Mind

The Lightworker's Guide to Getting Started

The Lightworker's Guide to Grounding Energy

"I CAN BE" Patterns of Purpose: Color Your Way to a Better You

Spiritual Ass Kicker's Discovery Deck Oracle Cards

Annabel the Lost

